# FADED YELLOW BY THE WINTER

## SCOTT PEARCE

READING SIDEWAYS PRESS

First published 2019 by Reading Sideways Press
20 Tennyson Street, Richmond, VIC, 3121

readingsidewayspress.com
readingsidewayspress@gmail.com

Copyright @ Scott Pearce 2019

This book is copyright. Except for private study, research, criticism or reviews, as permitted under the Copyright Act, no part of this book may be reproduced, stored in a retrieval system, or transmitted in any form or by any means without prior written permission. Enquiries should be made to the publisher.

Cover design and illustration by Chris Rees
reesdesign.com.au

Other illustrations from *Follower*, the official organ of the Alberton Football League, Victoria – 1980, 1984, 1986

Typeset in Droid Serif 10pt

National Library of Australia
cataloguing-in-publication data is available
at http://catalogue.nla.gov.au

ISBN 978-0-6482610-4-9

Scott Pearce teaches English and Literature at Alia College and lives in Mooroolbark with his partner and their children. He received his PhD from Deakin University in 2016. He is a loyal supporter of the Hawthorn Football Club. *faded yellow by the winter* is his first novel.

## Acknowledgements

Many thanks to: the team at Reading Sideways Press, Andy Fuller, Nuraini Juliastuti and Chris Rees for their belief and hard work; Michele Fuller for proofreading; Maria Takolander, not only a great Supervisor but a guide and a support; Varuna, the National Writers House, for the opportunity to develop my work as a recipient of a Varuna PIP 2017 Fellowship; Croydon TAFE Professional Writing and Editing class of '97; Alia College and my Alian family of dreamers, idealists, freaks, weirdos and Super Vegans; Katja Gurney, for decades of support and friendship; Andrew "Ace" Politis, the most gifted footballer I have ever seen. An inspiring Captain on and off the field; Jeroen Matser, a lucky charm, a fellow Hawthorn supporter and a beloved January companion; Adam Callander and Dan Porter, for the unconditional friendship, support, editing, hilarity and good times (wink); and you Jessica McConnell, for the love, encouragement, companionship, and for our amazing kids: Charlotte, Harriet (and Catty), Sullivan and Matilda.

To
Mike and Kathy Pearce

# 1

Vic had not thought about the dream for many years. From the age of twelve, until just after he turned eighteen, the dream had occurred so frequently that he considered it banal and drab. Then it stopped. There was, as far as he knew, no provocation for its arrival or for its disappearance. Now, twenty-four years later, it had returned. He did not know what to make of it all those years ago and did not know what to make of it now. He was, however, surprised by how vibrant the dream had become.

It began with him in a pitch-dark room stepping cautiously forward, following a woman he could sense but couldn't see. Then a door opened to reveal a sunlit desert that was partly obscured by the silhouette of the woman as she hesitated, her left hand reaching up to gently touch the doorframe. The woman, he presumed, was emblematic of his mother and he had a sense that she was anxious, restless. Then she stepped out onto the veranda of a rough-hewn house. He went out too but stood away from her. Now he had an unbroken view of his vast surroundings. The desert was a marvellous wash of reddish sand, littered with patches of coarse flaxen coloured grass; but the sky, an ethereal blue, stirred in him a foreboding. In the far distance, he could make out immense sandstone buttes, shades darker than the sand and separated from each other by shimmering stretches of desert that crossed the horizon. He could not turn to look at the woman, but he knew she was watching the space between the buttes and he watched it too. He saw a horse and rider approaching and then the dream returned to pitch-dark.

There was a gusty rain on the ute's windscreen, but Vic opened the driver's door and skipped over to a band of tall pines. A lone yellow-tailed black cockatoo, caught in a high draught, crossed over the steep valley and he watched it turn and circle. By and by the cockatoo drifted closer towards the hill from where Vic looked down on the town of Henrithvale. If the clock tower that stood on the outskirts of town had been in working order, the twelve chimes of midday would have spread through the lowlands. From where he stood, Vic could see the sharp ridges behind his farm, but not the farm itself, not the waning white weatherboard house with its red tin roof, or the apple trees that were his charge. The wind mumbled something in his ears; he thought that if he were the cockatoo then he would surely see the disused train line, the station house, the withered Sterling River that skulked alongside it, and his father's tree. Perhaps he might also see the blessed football ground, and that would undoubtedly portend victory.

The cockatoo came nearer, trying to find sanctuary in the branches of the pines, but it was driven away by rolling squalls. Vic moved from under the cover of the trees and stood out in the open next to his ute; a rough rain battered against him. Up above, the cockatoo was patient, moving closer and then, reluctantly, farther away from the branches of the tallest pine. Its wings, stretched out from its body with a slight arch, braced as it waited for the brooding winds to relent. It reminded Vic of a boat caught in a tremendous ocean swell, unable to reach port; and he, a solitary observer, could do nothing more than hope for its safety.

The rain found rhythm as the rise and fall of thunder crossed the valley. The winds eased and the cockatoo settled into the overhead branches; although dishevelled it was unharmed. Vic was fascinated and observed as it perched and used its beak to rearrange its feathers and shake off the dusting of raindrops. He moved back under the cover of the trees where the sweet cinnamon smell of the pine needles was suddenly irresistible. He rubbed a boil on the trunk where sap had gathered.  There was no rain in the town, not yet, and if he were lucky it would pass right over. It had been the wettest winter Henrithvale had dealt with in seven seasons; it was good for the orchard, for the dams and for the river, but it had come too late. Now he just wanted the rain to hold off until after the game.

Vic took a breath, slow and deliberate, so that the mix of fresh rainfall and pine needles might linger in his thoughts for the coming afternoon. This was the place his father had come to in the hours before the liturgy and Vic continued the practice. He returned to the ute parked on the side of the track but was again drawn to the cockatoo. It rubbed its beak, this side and then the other, on the trunk of the pine. Then it stopped, lifted its head as if hearing some urgent dispatch, and plunged from the branch and into the rising winds. It turned away from Vic and tilted its wings so that it came hurtling back over his head, showing him its dull yellow tail feathers, and let out a raspy, ke-awww, ke-awww. Then it hurried towards an avalanche of swirling grey clouds descending from the east.

The bird dived and then swept towards town, over the green land and empty houses that had been homes in the days when the farms were prosperous; but he lost it in the haze. Then, briefly, he saw it again, or so he thought, as it turned beyond the football ground; then it was gone. The rain had dampened his clothes, but he felt prepared, as if the ball was already in his hands and the game was won.

— ★ —

By the time the ute found bitumen the rain had retreated, and Vic took his foot off the accelerator and let the ute roll down the sharp decline towards the township. His game bag was on the seat next to him and his left hand rested on top of it. He passed the Avenue of Honour, twenty-eight trees—Scarlet Oaks and Sugar Maples—planted to honour the twenty-eight Henrithvale men who had fallen in the Great War, most of them at Pozieres. The Sugar Maples were bare so that all the arteries and veins could be seen, but a few curled and browning leaves still clung to the Scarlet Oaks. Two of the trees were planted for his two great uncles; they stood next to each other, one leaning to the left and the other to the right. When in bloom the foliage of one could not be distinguished from the other. When Vic was eight, he had climbed one of the trees and his grandfather, with a battered and muddied face, bellowed at him to get down and then hit him, open palm, behind his left ear.

"Don't you ever climb in that bloody tree again or by God you'll know all about it!"

Vic didn't understand what he had done wrong. It was his mother who explained that the trees were to remember those who had died in the war, and that sometimes the living are beholden to the dead. The trees were tired now, but Brian Hennan made sure that the plaques were sharp and clean and that every ANZAC day, every Remembrance Day, each one had a poppy. The losses that those trees represented had resonated for generations; the sudden absence of so many young men was obscene and unreconcilable. Fewer men went to the Second World-War; there weren't as many of age and the ardent zeal to protect Empire and see the world had become an obligation. Still, there was a memorial in town for the dozen men who hadn't returned.

Beyond the Avenue of Honour, the road levelled out and the school was on the right; a three-room sandstone building in which he had spent his school years. It had been rebuilt after it suffered in the fires that nearly claimed the entire town back in the 1930s. Outbuildings, a playground and cricket nets had been added in the time since he went there. Now it was a school for his daughters, Emily and Sarah.

Vic had recently found himself spending an evening or two every week back in the school. Led by Brian Hennan, president of the Henrithvale Growers' Association, Vic, and the town's other farmers sat on small chairs and spent long hours discussing what to do about the government decision to requisition the water leases that irrigated their farms. Along with the requisition plan there were government offers - substantial offers - to buy out all the remaining farms in the area. There were rumours a dam was coming. But, Henrithvale wasn't the first town to be sentenced; there had been others further up the valley that had already been devastated. Those individuals who didn't sell, those who would not concede, were worn down like rocks on the shore. Each week Brian cultivated the idea that the decision should be opposed, that it could be challenged and reversed; but only if they maintained opposition. He said the meetings were the cornerstone of a united front. The school itself was also under threat, subject to a feasibility study that had commenced in February. Yet it was never part of their discussions. Brian said they could not divide their forces, besides, the irrigation leases were the lifeblood of the town.

— ★ —

The ute rounded the broad road that took Vic into the town proper; there was still no rain, but the flat sunshine was frail.

None of the shops were open. People walked along the streets in club colours, worn like maroon vestments, on their way to the football ground. Vic stopped the ute on the side of the road near the general store, the last in a row of six late nineteenth-century former haberdasheries. A tall man in a grey suit came out of the store as Vic approached. He was holding a newspaper under his arm and he gave Vic a polite smile and held the door open for him. Vic thanked him and had a faint impression he knew the man, but he wasn't sure how. There was, as usual, a 'closed' sign on the store's door.

"Jack?" He called in his cowed baritone voice. "Ya there Jack?" From the rear of the shop Herbert Bannock materialised. Herbert had been called Jack his entire life, for his father and grandfather were both named Herbert. A short and lean man in his late seventies, Herbert did not seem, to Vic, to look much different than he did twenty or even thirty years ago.

"Here he is!" Herbert greeted him. "The man to bring sporting glory to all in Henrithvale!" Vic was chuffed.

"I'll be happy to getta kick, Jack."

Herbert had always encouraged Vic no matter what the endeavour. When Vic was ten, he had, for a short period, wanted to be an archaeologist and discover lost cities and grand treasures. Herbert had ordered archaeology magazines and displayed them near the door. When Vic came in after school, Herbert proclaimed:

"Here he is, the next Howard Carter!"

Herbert knew how much Vic had wanted to make football a career and had urged him to leave Henrithvale, but Vic knew he wasn't good enough and never gave the idea serious consideration. Vic's father, John, had spent a preseason training with Collingwood: The Purloiners, as Herbert called them. John came back home before the season was to begin and broke his leg in a motorbike accident. The leg wasn't set properly and when it healed it would not stand up to professional training. It didn't stop him from playing country football, but it meant he would never go any further. Vic remembered the way his father's leg would swell after a match, and the way he would limp around the house with ice, wrapped in towels, strapped to his ankle and tibia; a drip trail marking his travels.

Vic appreciated Herbert more now than he did as a child. His optimism, even poorly disguised, was a necessary diversion.

"How's Edna?" Vic asked, as he scanned the stale room and leaned against the counter. Edna, Herbert's wife, had cancer in her lungs after decades of cigarettes. She had a permanent odour of tobacco, whether she was smoking or not; it was something akin to the smoke from the burning of damp wood and pepper. Edna had come home from hospital the day before. In the last ten years she had been through two chemotherapy treatments and two operations. The cancer would go, but it always came back.

"Long drive, you know how it is." Herbert poked at the dust on the empty shelves. "She'll be up and around soon enough. She's upstairs, otherwise we'd be at the game." Vic nodded.

"I'll drop in after; let ya know how things went." He scanned the room. "You need anything, Jack?"

"How about a few more hours in the day?" Herbert lamented. He turned to face Vic. "Any more news on the farm?"

"Nothin'. Brian still reckons they're tryin' to scare us out. He reckons they won't go through with it."

"No one's selling?"

"Dunno, haven't heard anything. Brian thinks if we dig in they'll leave us alone."

"It's in the papers you know, all the way down in the city. I didn't think anybody would know where Henrithvale was. Look at this." Herbert moved in behind the counter and pulled out a copy of the city paper. The front page headline read, "Government faces increasing scrutiny over water buyback scheme."

"Haven't read it." Vic said taking the paper from him and reading the article.

"It says there is a lack of transparency in government motives." Herbert's droll smile became derision. "Who would've imagined it, lawmakers and legislators up to no good!" He sighed and cradled his jaw with his left hand. "Show it to Brian."

"Alright, no worries." Vic held the paper up in salute as he left and climbed back in the ute. In the rear-view mirror he saw the church across the road from the store; its windows boarded shut. It had been closed for years, but still held the occasional wedding or funeral. When Vic was younger it had been a meeting place; on Saturdays people gathered in the stand to watch Henrithvale play football, and on Sundays they gathered to hear the word of God. When the church closed, and services were moved to a bigger regional town, Herbert told him that God couldn't compete with football; a person could not worship in two different houses.

Vic drove through town and climbed a slight rise. The Royal Mail Hotel, positioned as it was across the road from the football ground, was doing solid business despite the early hour. The hotel, an enormous two storey sandstone building with wide covered verandas and a dome, was a lasting reminder of the gold rush boom of the 1850s. The boom established Henrithvale; there had been rich mines in the area that attracted people from around the world. At its height, Henrithvale had sixteen hotels, two train stations and a population some estimated at twelve thousand. Now there was one hotel and the train line was no longer in use. The mines, those that were known, served as a curious attraction to passing tourists. Vic had often frequented the mines with Dave Foster when they were teenagers. There were other remains of the gold rush too. Plaques commemorated the Chinese cemetery, a mine collapse that killed thirty-two, and the site of the town's first and only newspaper. There were stories wrapped in the lineage of those, like him, who could trace their forebears back to that time; stories of great fortunes lost and won, of Irish Catholics and Protestants warring in the mines so that the town introduced and enforced a selective 'No Irish' policy. Vic's grandfather told him some families were turned out of their homes or burned out and left with only what they could carry.

"That's history," his grandfather said. "Full of bastards who become saints." Beyond the mines were caves, near the sandstone quarry with its smashed outcrops, some of which still had ancient hand stencils and emu tracks.

– ★ –

Vic gave the car horn two quick taps, and the regulars on the second storey balcony of the Royal Mail brandished their pre-game beers. When he was a boy, the front bar was nicknamed "John's Place" after his father. He still heard people say, "I'm off to see John," when they were going for a drink. Vic turned left onto a partially sealed road that sloped towards the football ground. Cars were lined up to pay for entry. Vic didn't mind the wait as it gave him an opportunity to look over the playing field. Other cars had encircled much of the oval. On the far side, the Henrithvale Town Stand appeared nearly full. The football season had been a farce, a mockery of what it had once been. The Western Football League had boasted sixteen teams back in the early 1970s, but now the towns around Henrithvale were dying and their football teams were going with them. Last season there had been six teams in the league, but four teams had merged into two and that left the current league with four teams in total. They played each other three times with five byes to fill out the season.

Henrithvale had finished second on the ladder with six wins and three losses; although two of those six wins had been by forfeit. If they could beat Newfront today, they would play in a Grand Final for the first time in twenty-four years. Vic had wanted to win a Grand Final since he was a child. His father had played in ten, winning eight, including six in a row, and he had seen each one. He had watched his father hold the premiership cup high above his head and remembered the jubilation and the fervour of those around him; there was something transcendent and permanent in that experience he wanted for himself.

Brian Hennan was on the gate, selling entry tickets to cars and to those on foot as if he were offering benediction. He had been a striking ruckman from the late 1950s through to the mid-1970s when Henrithvale was dominant. Then, a building accident shattered the bones in his left leg. They were held together now with metal pins and he had limited flexibility at the knee. At the time people had joked he was trying to outshine John, and Brian had, initially, embraced the comparison. John, however, had not.

Now, Brian was overweight and slow moving, but always busy and always in a shirt and tie; he favoured light-blue shirts, short sleeved, almost transparent, and broad brownish ties. He wore small square glasses with a bluish tint and had his hair cut on the last Friday of every month. His nickname from his playing days was Clock, although no one called him that anymore. He coached the football team, was club president and was also president of The Henrithvale Growers' Association.

The ute pulled-up where Brian was standing, and Vic rolled down his window. The buzz of the public address system could be heard faintly in the distance.

"Are we that hard up, Brian, you've gotta coach as well as sell tickets?" Vic needled him, but Brian did not see the humour in it.

"Well, just for the time being, yes, we are. I had Master Mathews here, but he has taken off to who knows where, and people were getting in without contribution." Brian spoke in a measured and formal tone. A boy with hunched shoulders came sheepishly towards the gate. "Well, here is the young man in question!" Brian announced and began a familiar lesson. "When you are entrusted with a task like this, you are given a responsibility, and it becomes a measure of your character. I am relying on you, and so is everyone else in Henrithvale."

"Sorry, Mr Hennan, I had to go to the toilet." Brian gave the impression he was weighing up the boy's virtue.

"Be that as it may, Master Mathews, you have a job to do—" Brian was interrupted by a voice of discontent, and Vic could see in the rear-view mirror there were three more cars waiting impatiently behind him. "Now, you have got another chance, young man, don't make me sorry I gave it to you." Brian handed the boy a coin pouch and a ticket book.

"C'mon, Brian, get in," Vic called, and Brian went around to the passenger door. As he did Vic handed the boy, no more than twelve, a five dollar note.

"There's two dollars for parking and three dollars for you." The boy was thrilled. Vic pulled his game bag over onto on his lap before Brian collapsed into the seat.

"You've rewarded the boy for not doing his job," Brian complained.

"Have a look at what's on the dash," Vic said gesturing with his head. Brian leaned forward and picked up the newspaper. He held it up directly in front of his glasses.

"Yes, well, it's not unexpected. Those baby-kissers are no doubt feeling the pressure. There never has been one of that sort, and never will be, that can withstand pressure."

"Baby-kissers?" Vic was bemused.

"Make no mistake here, Vic," Brian said pointedly, "they are looking for us to give up and go away. But we need to put it aside for this afternoon and focus on the task at hand." He put the paper back on the dash. It had been Brian's organisation and unabated faith that had bound the farmers together. He had spoken of little else to anyone, whether they wanted to hear it or not, since news of the water requisition first became known.

Vic normally parked next to the stand, but because the spaces there were taken, he turned the ute towards the back.

"Didn't think we'd get this many," he said coming to a stop

"This is finals football, Vic. We haven't seen much of it for some time now - but mark my words people have wanted it."

Brian climbed out of the ute, and Vic followed, holding onto his bag with both hands. To get into the clubrooms, they had to walk around to the front of the large open-faced stand. The stink of beer, reheated chips and rollicking voices always reminded Vic of the days, years, he spent here watching his father, the great John Whelan, play football; while his mother, Glenda, worked in the tuck shop. He wondered if he might find them here somewhere; he knew they would be keen to see him play.

Vic estimated there were five hundred people in the Henrithvale Town Stand. It was named for the efforts that the entire community made to have it erected in the mid-1920s. It stretched the length of the eastern side of the ground and was built of sandstone bricks. The corrugated iron roof only covered a third of the seating and on hot days you could hear it buckle and stretch. On days when it rained, the wind would drive the rain in, so that unremitting drips from the roof frame irritated spectators long after the drenching had passed. There was seating for a thousand people on wooden benches; at least that's what Vic had always been told. And he had been there when it had been full on Grand Final days and remembered the cacophony that would tangle around the stand, ricochet off the roof and pulse through his feet. On rainy days, he would often sit in the car and pound on the horn when Henrithvale kicked a goal. The windows would fog over and then the game would continue in his head; only he would no longer be watching the game, he'd be in it, running down the wing and kicking a long goal.

Brian put a hand in the middle of Vic's back and directed him towards the race that led to the clubrooms under the stand. Vic understood, and while Brian turned to engage in conversation with supporters, he made for the race. Vic heard a few voices call:

"C'mon, Little John."

Whenever he did something on the field that reminded people of his father, he would hear something like that; but he wasn't the player and wasn't the man, his father had been.

John Whelan had been tall and solid, but also quick and agile. He was a fearless player - the type people remembered and talked about for years after having seen him play. Vic was less than six-foot-tall, thickset and couldn't run at pace. He often misread the play, but his father could see the ball leave someone's boot and know just where it would land, how it would bounce and what he had to do to get it before anyone else. It wasn't a skill you could learn; it was just something you had, something inside you, something that made you better than others. Vic was reliable, he had some good games, but Little John was not a name that he wanted or a name he deserved.

In the clubrooms, preparations had started. The air was laden with a homemade ointment; an eye-watering mixture of eucalyptus, tea tree, and peppermint. The players rubbed it into their skin. Years ago, there was someone to do the strapping; making sure ankles, knees and shoulders would get through another game. These days, the players strapped themselves or each other and they moved about in various stages of readiness. Vic sat on the bench that lined the walls and dropped his bag at his feet.

When his father played, Henrithvale had seniors and reserves teams. Now, they pleaded with friends and neighbours to make up the twenty-two players required for a single team. Vic, at forty-two years of age, was more than twenty-five years older than the Pattison boys, Adam and Dean, neither of whom had finished high school. Yet he was still sixteen years younger than Doc, who would say at the end of each season that he was retiring but had not been able to convince himself of it. Here they all were on the same team, wearing the same maroon jumper with a blue yoke covering the shoulders and the HFC logo on the front.

Vic wondered if the other players— many of them farmers like him—had been as distracted as he was. Usually, Vic would obsess about every game. Football season was a plague of wonted contemplations. Even during those seasons when they hadn't won a single game, when there had been too few players to put up any resistance, there was still a belief inside him before each game. Vic knew that the water leases should be more important than a game of football. He knew that their loss would ruin families, ruin the town; but the longer he sat in the clubrooms the further away all those concerns strayed, and he felt, no doubt as others did also, that he was leaving some wretched place behind.

Dave Foster sat down next to Vic and appraised the room. Dave had grown up next door to Vic. They had both been raised as the lone offspring of fathers with deep ties to the town and had known each other since childhood. They had explored mines that they had promised to stay away from, they had camped and fished together on weekends and school holidays, had climbed into and around the quarry; and they had talked endlessly about what it would be like to be a footballer on TV. In their mid-teens they broke away from each other, not too far, but there was enough distance now that they rarely spoke of anything other than football or farming.

Dave's round shoulders and swollen belly disguised his dexterity and his love of a physical contest. His acne scarred face, busy eyes and tangled hair had barely changed in all the time Vic could remember; his arms were thick and strong, covered in tattoos that had been weathered by too much time outdoors. Vic knew him by his scent, a sickly blend of sweat and cheap soap.

"What d'ya reckon?" Dave said, his voice, always louder than it needed to be, filled with enduring mischief. "Might finally have somethin' ta show for the past twenty somethin' years." Dave pulled off his t-shirt and wormed his way into his tight-fitting maroon jumper. "Fuckin' thing has shrunk."

"Didn't we win somethin' in the juniors?" Vic asked, although he knew they hadn't.

"Nah, that was bullshit. They did the round-robin tournament and gave everyone somethin'. We never won nothin'."

"Didn't I kick ten goals, take a big grab, win us the game?" Vic asked, giving Dave space to respond in a casual and crude way that had long endeared him to his team mates.

"Yeah, ha ha, fuckin' hilarious," Dave sneered. "And everyone bowed down to my ten-inch dick." He rolled the jumper over his stomach and grunted. "It's a Grand Final if we win this today," he stated. "That's somethin' we've never had." Dave stood up and took off his pants. "Shorts better not have gone the same way as this fuckin' jumper."

"There has always been plenty of room in your shorts, Dave," Doc stated casually. There was a brief lull in the exchange. Dave sized Doc up.

"Poof."

Doc, Steve Wallace, had never been able to master clubroom clowning. He was the fittest person Vic had ever known. He was the only vet in the district, and he spent most of his days on the road. At the end of the year he was moving his practice to somewhere near Ballarat but would still service the area when he could. There just wasn't the work in the Henrithvale district anymore.

"If it was a two-team competition, they'd still fill the place," Doc offered.

Vic leaned back against the wall and thought out loud.

"Doesn't seem real." He watched Dave wiggle into his shorts.

"I'm gonna strangle a fuckin' nut in these things." Dave's face was pained. "Maybe someone's got spares." He hobbled gingerly away, and Vic got changed.

The room came to a relaxed order when Brian Hennan entered, and Vic joined the players as they stretched and clowned their way through some shadow boxing. Peter Weston, the field umpire for the coming game, came in to check fingernails and boots. He lived in Henrithvale and had played junior football with Vic and Dave, but when he lost a kidney in his teens, he took up umpiring.

Brian Hennan, with help from Dave, stood on a chair next to a chalkboard and the players pushed in close. Vic stood on the outside of the group. Under Brian's guidance they revised their game plan on the chalkboard Brian was so fond of: move the ball quickly, play-on at every opportunity, do the team thing.

"You've all heard it before; a week can be a long time in football. And a single game can be the beginning or end of what you might have strived for years to achieve." His hands were clasped together.

"I shouldn't have to tell you what is at stake today. It's been a tough year for Henrithvale. It's been a tough two decades for this club."

Brian's voice was resolute; his words coming in short bursts. "There are people. I don't need to name names." His face flushed red. "They think Henrithvale is finished! They think we should pack up shop and go home!" Brian, as a coach, had a poor sense of theatre; he brushed over the rising action, rushed the climax, botched the suspense of the falling action and wallowed in the denouement. But the players knew their roles and Vic could feel the words.

Their voices answered back:

"C'mon, Maroons!"

"What happens today," Brian demanded, "is that we show everybody just how wrong they are! Just what Henrithvale is made of."

Vic looked up at the photo of his father that watched over the room. Next to it was the honour board with a list of the club champions, back when they still gave the award out. His father's name was there fourteen times. Vic wore the same number on his back as his father—seven. Today, he needed some of his father's skill and courage. Henrithvale needed it too; just one game where he could be the player so many, including himself, wished he would be.

Then, suddenly he was moving, part of the whole, being pushed through the clubrooms with the others, down the race and outside onto the ground. The crowd cheered and car horns blared. The ground was familiar, and alive with the trace of newly cut grass; the sky, a dirty white, seemed like it might hold off the rain.

The playing group spread out. They went through their drills and then Newfront came out: a team Henrithvale had beaten twice already during the year, mainly because they were unable to field a full team. They had played both times with fifteen on the field instead of the regular eighteen and they had no one on the bench.

Today would be different; Newfront looked ready, for they too had seen little success over the years, and this was also their day of possibilities. There was no rivalry to speak of, no real animosity. Newfront, after all, Vic knew, was just a variation of Henrithvale. He knew most of their players and they knew him, but, on game day, there is no camaraderie between teams.

Vic moved down into the forward pocket and crossed his fingers, hoping that today would be his day. Dave made his way into the centre and deliberately knocked into Newfront players, looking for the contact, wanting them to know he wasn't afraid.

When the teams were set, Peter Weston slammed the ball down into the centre of the ground to start the game; and it boomed like a single beat on a great drum. Adam Pattison tapped the ball down to Dave, who kicked quickly into the forward line. Doc, attempting to mark, was taken high. He took the free from forty-five metres out and kicked the first goal of the match before thirty seconds had passed. Vic found himself running towards the huddle of Maroons that had gathered around Doc, pushing into each other, urging each other on. The first quarter went their way. Adam Pattison dominated in the ruck, Dave Foster moved the ball forward and Vic provided decoy leads and shepherds to make room for Doc who was marking strongly. At the end of the quarter they had kicked eight goals and were up by seven. Vic, however, hadn't touched the ball.

At the quarter-time huddle, the supporters teemed from the stand and onto the ground. Vic felt their presence around him like a rising pressure. They needed something, something they could not articulate; but they knew it had to do with that ground and the jumper and the players. Brian Hennan started to speak; he was focussed and confident in his game plan as his tie fluttered and turned in the breeze.

"Alright, we are moving terrifically. Doc is getting plenty of the ball."

Voices called out encouragement.

"Now," Brian continued, "we need to start to find other options. They'll work to shut Doc down; we need to let them think we'll go to him every time we go forward. We won't. Dave Foster, you'll rest this quarter in the forward half and Pattison, the Adam variety, will go back. That puts Dean in the ruck. Vic, come off and have a rest." Vic knew it was coming; it was always the same. Players squashed in, and the racket of their voices covered Brian's final message. Vic felt the familiar shame of helplessness as he went to the bench, but as Brian shuffled to the coach's box, he was also reminded that coaching would always be a poor substitute for playing.

Vic was always a better player before a game when there was a chance to do the things he had so long imagined he could do. Years ago, he had reconciled his feelings with the mantra of "One day you'll find your game. Everything you've been looking for will be there. Just keep looking." It was a good philosophy; every week was one more chance. From the bench he could hear the bedlam in the stand like a storm about to engulf the game. Henrithvale kicked the first two goals of the quarter and then Newfront kicked five in a row.

At half-time, Henrithvale still had a solid lead. The players paused near the boundary line before entering the race to the clubrooms. Vic stood away from the huddle, stretching his hamstrings, so that it seemed his choice to be apart. Dave addressed the group.

"We dropped our heads. The game's not fuckin' over yet. Don't start thinkin' about what happens next week. Think about the right here, the right fuckin' here and now!"

"C'mon Maroons!" Vic called out. It sounded odd, poorly timed. He moved closer to the huddle but could not bring himself to lean in.

"Newfront? Pack of weak cunts!" Dave described every team that Henrithvale played in this same way. "When we hunted the ball, they didn't get near it. They kicked goals coz we fuckin' let 'em!"

Brian Hennan stood at the back of the group, willing to stomach the profanity when a game needed to be won. When Dave had finished, Brian led the players up the race for the half-time break. Vic was last in; a fraud and intruder. Christ. If he could just get a few touches. As he sat down on the bench, he could feel the photo of his father dissecting him, telling him to do better. He wanted it himself, but desire was nothing more than unrequited longing. He drank some water and Brian reviewed the details of the first-half.

Dave had squeezed out of his jumper and was standing bare-chested, eating an orange quarter. His left hand on his hip and then he spotted Vic.

"We need you in the second half, Vic." Then Dave held the orange in his mouth and squeezed both of Vic's shoulders with his strong hands.

"Yeah." His response was stiff. He stood up, faced the wall and simulated stretching until Brian readied the team for the second-half.

"Alright, up and about. Let's get going," Brian instructed. They started running on the spot, calling out encouragement. "In tight," Brian commanded. The players pushed in so close that Brian's face was no more than a few inches away from their own faces. Vic was in the middle, Dave's arm across his shoulder.

"We know what we need to do. In this quarter we shut the gate and put the result beyond chance. Don't let the horse bolt."

"Let's do it, Maroons. C'mon!" Vic closed his eyes and believed.

The third quarter started with Vic back on the field working to protect Doc. The ground was rough now, and the turned earth reminded Vic of the anxious dreams that haunted him during his childhood. He was on a football field, chasing a ball, opposition players closing in on him, but he could not run and could not do what John did. He rubbed some dirt between his hands; the rain was close.

Newfront were up and about now. Vic could sense their desperation. They took control in the centre. The banter started and as usual it was targeted at Dave; the same barbs. Just part of the game.

"Gee your wife's an ugly bastard, Foster. I wouldn't have kids either." Dave wasn't one for this type of talk, neither was Vic. The Henrithvale philosophy had always been: 'we don't start it, but we do finish it.' As the quarter went on Adam Pattison tired and couldn't give the Henrithvale midfield first use of the ball. Vic could sense it; it was in the way the Newfront players were breathing. They were no longer wheezing but hauling in long and abrasive snorts of air. Newfront kicked an early goal and a few minutes later added another.

The runner came out to Vic; it was the Mathews boy that Vic had seen working the gate.

"Coach says move up to the centre, create space for Dave." He stared at Vic waiting for an answer.

"No worries."

Vic ran up to the wing and waited for play to restart. Dave saw him and pointed to a Newfront midfielder who had started to control clearances from the centre, the one who had been doing a lot of the talking. When the ball was bounced Vic readied himself and then came straight in, dropping his shoulder low, just as the Newfront player reached for the ball. Dave was behind the Newfront player and shoved him forward. Vic felt his shoulder go in under the man's ribcage and the blow sent him into the air. He dropped the ball, and

Dean Pattison got to it first, shrugged a tackle and kicked a goal from beyond fifty metres.

The Newfront player, now lying flat on his back, didn't move; Vic could hear him trying to suck air into his lungs as he stood over him.

"Shut ya fuckin' mouth," he advised and dug his studs into the fallen player's outstretched fingers. Someone grabbed Vic from behind, flung him to the ground, and pushed his face into the mud; its dankness was in his mouth and he couldn't see what was happening. Players from both teams wrestled with and pushed at each other.

Vic clawed at the arm around his neck. Then he heard Dave's voice.

"Fuckin' cunt!" The arm and the offending player were gone. Vic rolled onto his back as Peter Weston manoeuvred in with exaggerated movements to separate the teams as they continued to shove and threaten each other. The long-haired and thick-bearded Newfront ruckman, pointed at Vic.

"Report that fuckin' prick!" he demanded.

"Have a sook, mate." Dave encouraged, and the Viking-like ruckman shoved him.

"It was a fair bump," Peter responded, but there was doubt in his eyes.

"Bullshit!"

Vic stood up; the exhilarating clash made the game sharper.

"That's abuse," Peter interjected. "Anymore and you're off."

The two teams continued to jostle.

Peter yelled:

"You can either play football or you can take this elsewhere." He blew his whistle to signal time on and the players scattered back to position. The Newfront midfielder that Vic collected, supported by trainers, left the ground.

"Vic, stay on the wing and run forward," Dave instructed as he darted past. When the game restarted, the Newfront ruckman went straight into Adam Pattison without going anywhere near the ball, knee to the hip, and gave away a free kick. Dave grabbed the loose ball and ran out wide.

"Advantage! Advantage!" Peter Weston called. Vic sprinted forward. He felt strong, his hands were dry and ready for the ball. Doc led out towards Dave, taking the defenders with him, but Dave kicked a high ball that cleared Doc and landed right in front of Vic. He gathered the ball, steadied and put through an easy goal from fifteen metres out. It was the third goal he had kicked that season.

He pumped his fists above his head before his team mates to share the celebration. They grabbed hold of him, as if he had surfaced after being under water for too long.

The game turned again. Henrithvale added three more goals and led by six at the end of the third quarter; it was lost for Newfront and the players on both teams knew it. As the Newfront players ran to their huddle Vic could sense the desperation in their voices. They called to each other: "We're still in this!" "Heads up!" They had to say it, Vic knew. He had done the same thing many times. You had to pretend you could win, even when you knew that you wouldn't. You said those things for your team mates.

The Henrithvale huddle was as thrilled as Vic had ever seen. Players patted each other on the back, but Brian Hennan wasn't impressed.

"Just in case any of you have forgotten, this is a four-quarter game! Enough of this rot, and a bit more focus. We're not home yet. Don't be remembered as the fools that got so far in front they couldn't possibly lose, and then managed to do just that."

The players gathered around Brian and the people of Henrithvale, carried on the currents from the stand, with their own desires for a win, once again surrounded the team.

The complexion of the day changed, and Vic felt the first fat drops of water that descended from low and distended clouds; a thunderstorm was coming. The last quarter would be played in the wet. It would hold up the play and work to their advantage. Brian's words were now competing against the high-pitched promise of lightning that threatened overhead. The siren went to signal for players to move into position; then came peals of thunder and a sharp pop that caused Vic to search the skies. There was lightning nearby, but nothing would force the players from the ground now.

"Finish what you started!" Brian demanded as torrential rain began.

As the last quarter started, the rain made it difficult to see and the ball seemed bogged in the centre square. Occasionally it moved into the Henrithvale or the Newfront forward line, but like a pendulum it soon swung back the other way. The players were tiring. The ball was too greasy for clean possession and too water-logged to travel any great distance. Neither team scored for twenty minutes. It would be a Henrithvale victory, it was assured, but it had an anticlimactic feel.

Vic waited in the forward pocket, his opponent next to him, but most of the onlookers had pushed to the rear of the stand. A tall man in a slate grey suit, sheltered by a large black umbrella, had stayed next to the fence. Vic remembered him from the general store earlier in the day and it felt to Vic that the man was not watching the game but was watching him.

Then, unexpectedly, there was an eruption of anxious voices and movement. The ball had been battered and pushed into the Henrithvale forward line. Vic was slow to react and his opponent led him towards the ball. Dave was coming from the opposite direction, but he had no intention of taking possession. He dived onto the swampy ground with a slap and slid on his belly, swinging his arm at the ball and knocking it further forward. The ball slid past Vic's opponent and into Vic's hands. He turned to kick but was hemmed in by two Newfront players. Hurriedly he handballed the ball away and then with five others set out in pursuit of it.

No one could take clean possession and the ball moved closer to the boundary line. Vic thought it would skid out of play, but a Newfront player managed to fumble it onto his boot and get a kick away as Doc slung him to the ground. Doc's tackle affected the kick and the ball skipped once and landed in Vic's hands; he kicked instinctively towards goal, knocked to the ground as he did so. The ball spun and turned and crossed the goal line to give Henrithvale the only score for the quarter. Vic was swarmed by his team mates; he imagined a younger version of himself watching the game, captivated by the events.

A few minutes later the final siren sounded and the Henrithvale players celebrated their victory. Vic's opponent, despondent and alone, held out a hand. Vic shook it as custom demanded, but they said nothing. Then Vic ran over to his team mates who were already embracing each other and making whooping noises. They left the thrill of the field with their arms around each other. Dave put his arms around Doc's neck in playful rough-housing, then kissed Doc's balding head. As they approached the stand, the crowd cheered and yelled their praise.

Vic heard the calls:

"Go, Little John! Go you good thing!"

He jogged, head down, up the race and into the clubrooms, no longer feeling misplaced; today he had played well.

The players formed a circle, arms around each other's shoulders or waists, feeling each other's greasy skin and savouring the sweat and mud that covered their bodies. Brian Hennan, beset by a fury, pushed into the middle of the circle and, waving his arms, more like a drunk boxer than a conductor, roused the players into the team song.

"We all stick to the Blue and Maroon." Vic and his team mates joined in with exuberant voices.

"Win or lose, Henrithvale don't change their tune;
That's the team we hold so dear,
We'll be Premiers this year;
And you'll see us with the Pennant very soon."

The song finished with a triumphant roar and the players set upon Brian so that he soon appeared as if he too had been out on the field.

Gradually, they began their post-match rituals. Dave removed tape from his ankle and shoulder, screwed it into a ball and threw it at Brian. Soon others joined in, Brian scolding them but unable to contain his joy. They relived important moments of the game they had just played with different thoughts and perspectives. Doc pointed at Vic and said the game turned when he "took care" of the Newfront player that had been winning the ball in the middle. Dave leaned over and affectionately rubbed the back of his head.

Vic wasn't sure what to say. He knew the man in the photo on the wall above would approve, but he could not bring himself to check.

Gradually, alone, or in small groups, Dave and the others undressed and went into the showers, where Vic knew they would stop being together, stop being the Henrithvale Maroons and return to their normal lives. Vic was the last to go in; he sat for a long time with his head down, staring at the floor as he replayed the game highlights in his mind.

# 3

It was verging on evening when Vic drove away from the ground. The rain had not subsided, and it led him to wonder if Jane and the girls had come to the game. That morning Jane put forward a loose idea of seeing her mother, and he hadn't asked for details. If they had been at the game, Vic thought, Emily and Sarah would have been waiting for him outside the clubrooms; he could always count on his daughters to laud his efforts, regardless of the score. He decided that he would share the victory with Herbert and Edna.

The general store was closed, and a quivering street light reflected in the windows. There was nothing on the shelves. Vic tried the door, which was still unlocked, and made his way inside. He called out to Herbert and then ventured into the back of the shop, through a hallway and into the adjoining house.

Herbert and Edna were sitting at a small table in the box-shaped kitchen, resplendent with 1950s décor and complete with a lonely wood burner stove that provided oppressive heating. Herbert was feeding Edna a watery soup. Her skin was grey with a slight blue tinge and her clothes had been washed in hospital antiseptic. Vic knew she was sick, but this was worse than he had expected. Herbert stood up when he saw Vic.

"Sit down, Jack, for goodness sake. It's Vic." Edna's voice was still hers; a kind and coarse sound worn down by use.

Herbert did as Edna demanded, resting his left hand on top of hers.

"Sit down, Vic," Edna insisted. "Now, by the hullabaloo going on outside, I think we might have won a game." Vic beamed and sat down at the table.

"Yeah, won comfortably, Ed. Rain helped get us home."

"Well, a bit of rain won't hurt anybody, will it? Not before time either." She started to cough and wheeze. Herbert put a hand on her back.

"It's all right, it's all right," she said, taking a few difficult breaths. "I'm only dying."

"Hang on for a bit longer will you, Ed?" Vic asked. "You'll see a premiership next week."

"And I'll die happy if I do, I can tell you that for nothing." She patted his hands as they rested on the table.

When Vic was a boy, Edna was the Henrithvale Football Club matriarch. Herbert and Edna's youngest child, a boy called Oliver, had been an eager and talented footballer. Vic knew him from a single photograph that was kept in their bedroom. Edna often talked about him, but Herbert never did. He died when he was ten, hit by a car while riding his bike. The car didn't stop and nobody saw it. It happened the morning after a Henrithvale Grand Final win. It was, most likely, someone from the town, but no one said anything. No rumours, no speculation.

After Oliver's death, Herbert and Edna made the town their focus. It was Edna's efforts that got the tuck shop built onto the side of the stand. She organised the raffles, washed the jumpers and kept the club prosperous. Vic didn't think about it when he was younger and couldn't make sense of it when he was older. The year the cancer first hit she was voted club champion. There was a picture of her with some of the players on the front page of the district paper. It was the first time anyone had heard of someone winning such an award without playing a single game, but that was years ago. Aside from him, Vic didn't know anyone from the club who visited her now.

"What are you doing with that farm of yours, Vic?" Edna demanded, seeming to gain strength.

"He'll sell the bloody thing if he has any sense," Herbert answered, but there was no drive in his words. He was a tired actor.

"There's a Growers' Association meeting tomorrow, Brian thinks if we stick together it'll work out."

"Don't worry about what Brian thinks. What do you think?" Edna had always wanted to know how he saw matters or what he thought. When she had been strong she would put her hands on her hips if he did not answer and demand that he share his opinion.

He stared into the bowl of soup cooling in front of Edna and then down at the floor.

"That farm, the apples…" His voice disappeared.

"What about Jane and the girls?" There was no respite from Edna once she had decided he hadn't fully considered an issue.

"Probably just wait and see." He leaned back in the chair.

"You just do what's best, won't you? Be worried but don't be afraid." Edna started coughing again; a shuddering sound.

Herbert rubbed her back. Vic was sure that this bout of cancer would pass, just like the others had. Edna had been told before that her time was coming to a close. The doctors had been wrong then; no doubt they were wrong now.

"I'll head off home, then back to the Royal for a drink." Vic stood up and held out a hand to Edna. She took it, and he felt the clamminess and thinness of her skin and thought it might rip if he pressed it too hard. When he took his hand away, he could see the points where his fingertips had been; what remained was a reddish-purple indent that would come to a bruise.

His father would have said that it needed ice to keep the swelling away. He used to say that bruises always looked much worse than they were. When the crimson faded to beige, he would say there was no real harm done and he would dismiss the injury as if it was not then, nor ever should be, of any consequence.

Outside, the gutters could not contain the run-off and leafy debris was swept onto the footpath. The wind shoved at Vic as he scurried to the ute and drove towards the farm; the windscreen wipers scratched and squealed as they dragged back and forth across the windscreen. He wondered if Jane would be home. He thought about their conversation last night; the same one they had been having for the past seven months. She wanted to sell, take the government offer and move somewhere closer to her parents.

Jane had moved to Henrithvale when they married, more than ten years ago. She'd had enough now of Vic's trust that everything would work out. He had tried to explain why they needed to stay but she didn't want to listen, didn't see it his way, not anymore. They were tired conversations in the hours after the girls were asleep, and Vic thought they had both talked the words out of it. Lately the discussions were more accusatory, more about them, about him, about choices. He worried they would wake what was better left alone. She was nineteen when he met her, he was thirty-two. He hadn't thought much about getting married or having kids. Until Jane he'd never really had a girlfriend, just the occasional drunken romp with seasonal fruit pickers: girls he knew would leave soon enough and were unlikely to return. He had been content with lonesome introspection, but Jane found a way in. She was instantly engaging, almost maternal, and that quickly transformed into a benevolence that comforted the thoughts that had long kept him from closeness with others. She used to say how much she loved his restraint, his stoicism, but not anymore; now he was short-sighted and impractical.

"You can't make decisions just for you, Vic," she had said last night. "We've got to make decisions for our family." All this talking exposed a space that had opened between them and it was unclear how wide it had become; the requisition of the irrigation leases had released an inner turmoil and Vic, unable to contain it, had fallen back on inherited habits that made him wary and apprehensive. It was the school closure that worried her the most, but he thought she was being alarmist and had sided with Brian.

Still, it was difficult enough before the threat of school closure and the requisition letter: there were ongoing negotiations with the bank to restructure or suspend repayments, and there were bills that just couldn't be paid. There was never enough money to stop the worry. She couldn't handle the stress of it and borrowed from her parents at times. Vic pretended he didn't know. The way she saw it, the requisition was a gift. Here was the government offering him a touch over half a million to just walk away. What she didn't seem to fully understand is that he wouldn't be just signing away an irrigation lease, but more than a hundred years of the past and everything built on that.

Vic had grown up in Henrithvale on the same farm as his father, his grandfather and his great-grandfather. The kitchen table had been crafted from local timber by his great-great grandfather and bore the markings of each generation. The table was recognisable in the background of photographs taken fifty and even a hundred years ago. He didn't want to be the one who couldn't manage the heartbreak and the relentless work, the one who gave it up. There was something wrong with turning your back when things got too hard.

And yet, Jane, he worried, was right. The state and federal governments had been elected on a platform of rebuilding the country's waterways, protecting its forests and finding a new way to generate wealth. The Sterling River was stressed, some said irreparably damaged, and in parts further downstream it didn't flow during summer. The impact on communities beyond Henrithvale, as well as on the flora and fauna, had been compelling; there wasn't enough water for everybody. Some people blamed the Greenies, born and bred in the city, dictating how to manage land and water they'd never touched. Maybe. But Vic knew it wasn't the Greenies selling land to idiots who wanted to grow thirsty crops like cotton and almonds. It was a little bit of everything. Now the government was actually doing something with the requisition of irrigation leases all along the Sterling River. It wasn't a major river, and Henrithvale wasn't a big farming community compared to those on the Murray or the Darling. That was no doubt why the Sterling River became the focus: it was big enough to make it seem like something was being done and small enough that impact on large primary producers wouldn't be significant.

Vic also worried that, if he couldn't find a way out, in the end, it would come down to the farm or Jane; and Jane would take the girls. He thought it was the isolation that had got to her; not just on the farm but in the town. There were times when he was younger, on school holidays, when he wouldn't see anyone else but his mother and John for days. He would fish the river or scout the old train line that crossed the hills beyond the farm, satisfied with his own company and his own frontier. These days he could always find something that needed his attention, something that took him away from the house and made it so he got home too late.

He knew Jane was lonely: football games, working in the tuck shop and washing dirty football jumpers had lost its appeal. You could never be a local, never really be of Henrithvale, or understand what that meant, without the generations that tethered you to the past. Jane didn't have forebears, blood in the ground, and sacred items passed from one generation to the next. She had no real claim.

The rain made it hard to see and then a savage and unsettling lightning burst on an outlying hill lit up the open fields for a split second. The ute came up over a sharp incline, where the bitumen lapped at the edge of the gravel road, and then drove down a long straight stretch. His headlights caught a glimpse of the lone gum, his father's tree, some forty metres from the road; a monstrous and irrevocable mark on the landscape.

Vic leaned into the bend and then the road straightened out again. He could see the veiled lights from the house in the distance. Jane and the girls were home. Maybe he was wrong; maybe she had seen the game. Maybe she had taken the girls down to see the end of it and came home to avoid the bad weather.

Again, lightning bore down from the sky and Vic thought he saw two men by the side of the road. They waited in the long grass; their faces partially covered by broad brimmed hats. He thought he knew them. Another lightning flash revealed nothing but a few saplings and a wall of English Broom. He took in a careful breath; it was a trick of the light. Nothing to worry about. This was the day he had wanted; the day he had been waiting for. Henrithvale was into a Grand Final and he was finally part of it. He wished his father had lived long enough to see it. If they won the cup next Saturday he would take it to the cemetery and show the old man.

Vic turned into the winding driveway that curled first to the right and then the left. The ute's headlights showed the mature apple trees on the right side, before turning to the three-year-old trees on the left. The thunder was working its way down the valley, like seams coming apart.

The ute came to a stop in the carport at the back of the house. Vic saw glimpses of Jane through the kitchen window. She was talking to somebody—though he couldn't see who. He turned off the engine. The back door opened and the tall man in the slate grey suit strolled out into the porch light. He unfastened a large black umbrella.

Vic got out of the ute, his game bag hanging over his shoulder, and stood on the corner of the carport. The tall man seemed to know right where he was and came directly over and extended his right hand. As if by compulsion Vic clasped it in his own. The tall man's grip was stronger than expected; his hands had known labour, they had been strained, nicked and blistered, until they had hardened. They reminded Vic of John's hands.

"Mr Whelan, I presume?" The voice was affable: it had a hushed Irish accent that was soothing and melodic.

"That's right." Vic leant back on the ute.

"Now I suppose you must be wondering just what I am doing here at this late hour." Vic didn't know how to answer. The tall man gave him the same uncomfortable feeling that he had felt earlier. "Don't be alarmed Mr Whelan, I am William Mulholland. I just came out here to discuss the requisition of the water leases—"

The wind pushed in under the carport and the roof reverberated against the frame.

"You're from the government?" Vic wondered how long he had been speaking to Jane and what she had told him.

"I'm not here to cause any distress, Mr Whelan." He rested the shaft of the umbrella against his shoulder and turned it slowly. "I'm just here to answer any questions you might have regarding the very generous offer that has been made for your land."

"Didn't think you blokes worked on Saturdays."

"It's a unique case Mr Whelan, and—"

"Call me Vic," Vic interrupted.

"Certainly." Mulholland smiled. "As I was saying, as I was just telling Jane," he motioned back towards the house with the tip of the umbrella, while keeping his eyes on Vic, "a unique situation requires a unique approach. Now, tell me, Mr Whel—Vic, do you—"

"We're not interested." Vic stood up straight. He could see his breath in the night air as the strain of the day's game awakened in his legs and shoulders. Mulholland's genial demeanour remained.

"I am not here to turn any screws, Vic. No doubt there are questions you have that need answers. Jane was certainly interested in possibilities," Vic glanced at the kitchen window and Mulholland paused as if troubled, then spoke diplomatically. "I think our conversation together has her better prepared."

"No one's gunna sell. You can talk to whoever ya want." Vic's voice had an unintended bravado that sounded like juvenile defiance.

"Okay, okay," Mulholland relented. "There's certainly a lot to think about, but Vic, don't mistake my purpose. I am only here to answer questions."

"Well, I don't have any," Vic lied.

Mulholland seemed pleased. He made as if to leave, but then, unable to resist, turned back.

"Do you mind, Vic, I am curious to know something."

"What?" He adjusted the bag on his shoulder.

"Your family's been here a long time, haven't they?"

"Hundred and thirty years, give or take." He liked the hallowed connection.

"Magnificent history," Mulholland said and bowed his head as in admiration. Then he contemplated the blackness as if to take in the landscape. "And you've never lived anywhere else? Never wanted to see the world as they say?"

"Not really, no."

"I was born in Belfast, Ireland. Perhaps the accent is a giveaway?" Vic found something appealing in Mulholland that he couldn't resist. "I left home when I was a lad, just fifteen. Sailed all over the Atlantic for years, gave it up and landed in America. Imagine that, a boy from Belfast joins the navy, sails the Atlantic and ends up in America as a zanjero." His eyes dug in and Vic felt suffocated, as if there was no space between. "It's a big world, Vic; don't miss your chance to see it. You won't get another."

"Maybe one day." He peered towards the back door. The rain, urged on by the thunder, was almost insufferable. "I need to get in."

Mulholland stopped turning the umbrella and lifted the shaft off his shoulder. "Take those pretty girls of yours and show them the world. They'll learn more from that than in a classroom; but don't let me hold you up. I'll bid you good evening and wish you congratulations on the hard-won game today."

"No worries." They shook hands again. Mulholland reached into the pocket of his waistcoat and took out a pocket watch. He squinted at it, then disappeared into the murky night.

Vic wondered where he had parked, maybe out on the road, but it didn't matter. He hurried toward the house and pulled the back door open. He took Jane by surprise: she turned from the kitchen sink with a gasp. Emily and Sarah danced around him, each with curled blonde hair knotted by a day of play.

"Hi, Daddy," Sarah said, her voice rising in pitch and her eyes bursting with eagerness. "Guess where we went today?"

"Shopping with your mother." Vic answered eyeing Jane and taking in the salty heat of fish-and-chips, their wrapping partially stuffed into the bin.

"Hey, how did you know?" Sarah put her index finger to her chin. She was the younger of the two. Jane had turned away from him.

"What did ya say?" It came out as a demand rather than a question. Jane, who was drying dishes piled next to the sink, kept her back to him.

"How about, 'Hi Jane, how was your day? Nice to see you.' That would be a good place to start." She spoke quickly, with needling and agitated inflections and didn't take her eyes off the plate in her hands.

"Daddy, I have new shoes. See?" Emily held up her leg to show Vic.

"Emily, I'm just talkin' to mum right now. You need to say excuse me if—". He struggled to hide the unrest in his thoughts. He felt himself widening his stance, bracing for the contest.

"Excuse me," Emily said graciously. He wanted to tell her to go away so he could talk to Jane, but he remembered himself in this very kitchen with his own mother. He knelt down.

"Wow! I bet you could run fast in these."

"They won't fit you, Daddy." Emily laughed.

"I can run faster," Sarah said pushing her foot up onto Vic's knee, so he could see her new sneakers too.

"Not faster than me," he said, watching Jane.

"I'll show you what else I got," Emily said and bolted out of the room.

"Me too," Sarah dashed after her big sister. Vic stood up.

"How was your day?" he asked hoping for a truce. Jane laid her tea towel on the dishrack.

"Busy. Busy and expensive," she was flustered. "Thought you'd stay out for a drink."

"Might go back to the Royal Mail, if you're interested? We're through to the Grand Final."

"Oh congratulations!" She kissed him on the cheek. "I don't want to take the girls out in this," she said, her head turning towards the window. "You go, though." Emily and Sarah came back in the room carrying their collection of new clothes.

"Look, Daddy." Emily held up a pink T-shirt with a fairy on the front. She wanted everything to be pink, just like Jane.

"I think the whole town's there," Vic said to Jane. "The girls'll be fine. Bundle 'em up. We'll take your car." There were brochures on the kitchen bench from the university in Bendigo. Shopping is what she had told him in the morning. He picked up one of the brochures and could feel Jane's eyes on watching him as he did. Nursing degree; something she had mentioned a year or more ago, but it had soon passed. Thunder vibrated through the house and the lights faltered and then held.

"Daddy, look." Emily was demanding.

"Mine's green." Sarah held up her new T-shirt. He was focussed on Jane and she kept her eyes on the brochure as he put it back down on the bench.

"Daddy, look!" Emily was irresistible. Vic knelt down in front of her and held up the T-shirt.

"Might fit me!" Vic frowned, and Emily giggled. "Maybe green is more to my liking." He took Sarah's T-shirt too. "Thanks, girls, I'll wear 'em to footy training." He went into the lounge room, the girls clinging to him and trying to retrieve their T-shirts. They climbed on him as he sprawled on the couch. He turned the TV on to watch the footy replay, but the picture was distorted and cut through with fuzzy lines.

"Alright girls, ice-cream time," Jane called and they left Vic alone and dashed back into the kitchen. A few minutes later Jane sat on a chair to his left.

"You're not going to the pub then?"

"Nup, don't feel like it." He kept focussed on the TV, despite the static interference. She waited for him to give ground, but he ignored her until she stood up to leave.

"If you're goin' to start talkin' to people about options," he said, turning the TV off, "you could let me know."

Any discussion with Mulholland would get out; he knew it would. Nobody would say anything directly to him, but he would see what they were thinking in their sighs, in the hesitation of their greetings. It would reach The Growers' Association, Brian Hennan, and others. She should have told Mulholland to come back later; she should have asked Vic what he thought. It would look bad.

"There was an open day at the university. I didn't know until we got there. Mum said something about it, so I stopped in." He wasn't sure what she was talking about. "Sorry, I thought we'd get back for the last quarter." The brochures.

"What did you say to—" Thunder stretched over the house and plunged them into black. They waited, anticipating the lights would return, but they did not. The girls called out for Jane, and she reassured them as she felt her way back into the kitchen. Vic got up to light candles. Storms often cut the power. He remembered the thrill of it as a kid; when the house became a cave to be explored and the monster could not find you.

Vic awoke to the morning light limping over the windowsill beneath the washed-out bedroom curtains. The bed next to him was empty. Jane must have stayed in with the girls again. A physical divide had edged in with their accusatorial exchanges and it kept them away from each other. The rain had stopped, and a faint musk invaded the house; it meant more rising damp. The phone was ringing, but he didn't move.

"If it's important, they'll call back," his mother would say.

His thoughts were focussed on how, in one week, he would play in a Grand Final. Then, quickly, he was pulled to the vase in the hall that people often admired and to the last time that Henrithvale had played in a Grand Final. Vic was a teenager. John's team had lost by six points, a single goal. They were supposed to win. It was the last game he had ever watched with his mother.

He remembered her lonely face on the drive home. John had stayed back at the club; he'd had a solid but unspectacular game. There wasn't disappointment in the Henrithvale rooms after the loss so much as a sense of being somehow conned and humiliated. His mother was already sick, but he didn't know how badly. She had told him that everything would be alright, that it wasn't serious, that he didn't need to worry.

John had come home late that night, leaving the headlights on in his ute so that they lit up Vic's bedroom window. It was the pounding on the unlocked front door, though, that had woken him. He heard his mother's voice trying desperately to calm John, ushering him to bed and then John's words shattered the windows; there was the brutal smack of his hand as it hit the side of her head, and she fell and knocked the vase off the stand in the hall. She used glue to put it back together, Vic held the pieces for her, but the cracks were there for everyone to see; although no one ever said anything.

He got out of bed when the phone rang a second time. Jane, her hair just washed, and her face worn from lack of sleep, met him in the kitchen as he was hanging up the receiver.

"It's Dave," he told her although she didn't ask. "He says there's a fence down."

After breakfast Vic put a few rolls of fencing wire in the back of the ute and drove along the track on the furthest side of the farm, where the irrigation pumps were. Dave had cattle in his top paddock and a break in the fence could send them into Vic's orchard. As he drove, Vic saw that the storm had done some damage to his trees, giving him more work to do. He still hadn't finished the winter pruning and he knew he would need another month or more to move through the whole orchard and adjust growth. On some of the older trees there were weak crotches and interfering branches he hadn't taken care of last winter. Now, there would be injured wood. He needed to look over every tree.

In past years he had hired help, but there wasn't the money for it now. He'd barely paid the pickers at the end of autumn. The ute stopped at the beginning of a steep rise and he got out. The ground was soggy and unstable, so he left the ute and continued on foot. He soon found the wire fence that separated his property from Dave's and he traced it over the incline. The earth was rocky, the topsoil too shallow to be of any use. There were patches of blackberry bushes here and there like islands, rabbit shit and the odd fox paw print in the mud. He had spent a lot of his childhood on this hill, and down in the gully behind which led to the old railway line and, further beyond, to some mining relics.

Vic heard Dave's quad bike and saw him coming up the hill on the other side of the fence and then come to a stop further up ahead by a large gap in the fence. The gap was almost ten metres wide, the fence posts and grass were partially burnt, and the wire fencing was frayed and ripped.

"Lightning?" Vic asked as he came up to Dave.

"Or the cows are gettin' smarter." Dave squatted down next to a fence post. "Wood looks alright. Got any wire?"

"In the ute," Vic signalled back over his shoulder. Dave rode the quad bike through the gap and kept pace beside Vic.

Vic recalled how, after school, and on weekends or holidays, he and Dave used to regularly come to the hill together. Vic's imagination in those days had been populated with dragons and elves, wild shoot-outs with horse thieves and treasure maps. Dave had always followed Vic's lead; he and Vic immersed themselves for hours at a time in epic tales. They had been kings and warriors, made brave defences and saved nations. Their games, so distinct in Vic's memory, made him uneasy now. He dare not mention them.

"Yer didn't come back to the pub ya lazy bastard," Dave complained. He had never liked silence.

"Power went out."

"Yeah." Dave guided the quad bike up next to the ute. "Hey, guess what Brian wants me to tell ya?"

"There's another meetin' tomorrow?" Vic answered with contempt. "You should tell him I'm busy. Got things on."

"Brian'd shit himself," Dave hooted.

They took the wire off the ute and worked to repair the fence, crouching to avoid kneeling on the sodden ground.

"You had any visitors?" Dave asked as he cut the broken wire away from the fence post.

"Visitors?" Vic wondered if Mulholland was speaking to everyone who was carrying debt. Vic knew that Dave owed money, not as much as him, but enough to be worried.

"Ya know, someone stoppin' over for a bit of a chat. A visitor."

Vic collected the broken wire, cleaned it on his sleeve and put it in his pocket.

"I know what a visitor is."

"Just checkin'." Dave moved to the other fence post. "I heard they send someone 'round to give one or two a better deal than the rest."

"More money you mean?" Vic asked

"Probably."

"Nah, no one has offered anything more than was in the letter." It wasn't a lie, not yet.

They threaded new lengths of wire and tightened them. Vic watched as Dave strained, his head tilted to one side and his left eye shut tight.

Just as Dave was finishing up, Vic saw there was smoke bleeding into the sky from the opening of a wound. He gasped, incredulous, as the smoke turned, mutating into half-formed horrors. The smoke, Vic knew, was from the old station house down through the gully and past the railway cutting. They were back, back at the station house, and he had to go to them. His hands clenched so he could feel his rough fingernails cut into his palms.

"What?" Dave asked turning to see what had taken Vic's attention. "Hey, Major Tom?" Dave clicked his fingers.

"I should see about things," Vic mumbled, waving Dave's hand away as the smoke approached, hunched and lurching.

"Yeah, alright." Dave sounded confused and scratched at his forearms in the way that told Vic he was worried.

"See ya at the meeting," Vic tried to reassure him.

Dave started the quad bike and rode away. Vic stayed where he was, and his legs felt as if they would give out. Then, with Dave gone, he made for the gully and the steep rail line cutting that he and Dave used to play in as children. He lost balance and toppled over as he began the descent into the gully and then stood up to brush the dirt and burrs from his pants. He had a surreal feeling of falling back in time.

There was a story that he had heard at school, as part of a local history project, about a robbery that took place on the road to Henrithvale in 1869. There was so much gold coming out of the ground in those days that the Bank of Victoria sent a special armed coach every two weeks to collect the gold from the Henrithvale branch and take it to the Bendigo branch. Sometimes the coach couldn't make the journey. During winter the road would be washed out, and the gold would accumulate in the small vault in Henrithvale.

In June of 1869 the coach from Bendigo had been delayed for several weeks. When it finally made the journey and collected the Henrithvale gold it was robbed on the way out of town by two Americans in collusion with three of the guards. The loot was divided in half, the Americans taking their half and riding back into Henrithvale to wait at the train station. A train to Newfront arrived before word of the robbery, and the Americans disappeared. The other half of the gold was taken by the guards, but they were caught a few days later and their ill-gotten gains recovered. Vic had found the station house by chance when he was eleven or twelve, on the run from John and desperate for a haven. It was at once familiar and when he entered nobody was surprised to see him. From that time on he would see the smoke in the sky maybe once or twice a week and would then be compelled to visit. A year after John's death it stopped.

He tripped his way through the blackberry bushes that had invaded the railway cutting. There were times when he could not be at home, times when John, poisonous and ferocious, would look for him. He would come here to the cutting and sometimes beyond to the station house where the two desperadoes had waited for the train. Any thought of ignoring the smoke, turning away or finding distractions was brushed aside by a consuming compulsion.

The cutting arched into a forested ravine and then flattened out. A patchy drizzle mulled about. He could see the station house now and the line of smoke winding from its chimney. He fixed his eyes on it and pressed forward.

The station house was unchanged: a solid sandstone building and bluestone platform. There was always something frightening about being here, but such feelings could not stop him.

Vic climbed onto the platform, put his hand on the door and took it away again. Then, unable to stop himself, he turned the door handle. The hinges on the door squealed and the room, like an old book left alone on the shelf for too long, was open. He saw them immediately—just as they had always been. The taller desperado was asleep, stretched out on a corner bench with his hat pushed down over his face, saddle bags at his feet. The other one, shorter and lean, with a sharp square jaw and a thick moustache, moved about, holding a rifle and checking the windows. He saw Vic come in, glared at him, and went back to the windows.

"Been some time since you come by," he said in a drawl and then looked Vic over more thoroughly. "Don't look like you starved none neither." He turned back to the window. "I suggest you find somethin' else occupy your time; gonna get real interestin' here real soon."

Vic wanted to know why they hadn't left, if they had been waiting here for him. He reached the door, but before he could push it open the lean desperado spoke again.

"Gonna sell that ranch then, that be the end of it?"

It was the same pattern. There had never been any talking around matters, no loose conversation to build rapport; the only words that were spoken were those that were needed.

Vic held his breath, and then he spoke.

"I can stay and go broke or leave and lose everything." He felt childish in the way he framed the situation, as if he had never been away.

"Lose everythin', you say? It's a damned way to put it." He kept his back to Vic.

"How would you put it?"

"I wouldn't go all-in on a single hand." The desperado chastised Vic. "No sir, all or nothin' is bad news."

"What is it then?" Vic did not think the desperado understood the complexities.

"Tell you what, move to the other side of the table and get another view of the game. You might just see somethin' a little different."

The taller desperado turned over and mumbled in his sleep something that Vic couldn't understand.

"You'd best not wake him. You know he ain't the type you wake unless it's a necessity." The lean desperado continued to move from one window to the next. "You take my advice and get goin'. Go on."

Vic hustled out of the station house, closing the door carefully behind him. The land was vast and empty; the sky was a grey desert, but the air was honied like water at the end of a long day. Then came that same feeling he had known before, every time he left this place, the urge, the need, to run, run and never look back. He lost his footing going down the platform steps, landed painfully on his hip, but got up and ran; his mouth filling with saliva, the wind bringing tears into his eyes. Behind him, Vic could hear the whistle and chug of the train as it neared the station.

Vic parked the ute and went inside. Jane was at the kitchen table, reading the brochure from the university open day. The house was quiet.

"Where are the girls?" he asked desperate to project an ease, a balance.

"With the Parker kids. Fence alright?"

"Lightnin' we reckon." Vic felt the kettle, still hot, and poured himself a coffee. "That's your plan then, is it, go off to university?"

"I don't know Vic, what's your plan?" She sounded tired, the fingers on her left hand massaged her forehead. Vic held an image of her as she had been when they first met. The marriage and farm had gradually refined her disposition, and now she seldom resembled the person he had married. He wanted a path back, but where and how to begin such a journey he did not know.

"There's a meetin' on tomorrow, probably know more then." He'd made similar statements every few weeks for months now.

"The school feasibility report will be out this week or next. What if the school closes? What then?"

"Can't do anything until we know. Wait and see, I guess." He wished he had a better side-step.

"Vic, what do you think's going to happen? What do you think we'll do?" She always emphasised the "you." He hated it, it was overdone. He sat down at the antique table, letting his hands clench the table leg. His thumbs traced generations of names engraved there. On your tenth birthday tradition held that your name would be carved into one of the legs; his name was there beneath John's name. He didn't have an answer that made sense, not to Jane.

"Brian thinks—" He began.

"Brian thinks this! Brian thinks that!" Her hands flew to the left and then the right as the frustration curled around her words.

He wished there was a known and single terrible event that had pushed them apart, something easily tracked and caught. The farm, the town—they were enough for Vic. He thought it would be enough for Jane. When they were married, barely six months after they first meet, she told him she couldn't be happier, that he and Henrithvale were what she needed. A few years in and something changed. Vic thought it was her parents, gnawing away at the foundations. They were overbearing, saw the marriage as a mistake and kept their distance from him. He thought her restlessness might pass, that as the girls grew up she would find a place for herself the way his mother had. She had tried working in town at the Royal Mail, but it wasn't enough. Whatever Jane wanted it didn't seem to be in Henrithvale, not anymore.

"There are some trees that need to be cared for," he said, running his right hand along the worn edges of the table.

He finished the coffee, said nothing else, put the cup in the sink and went back to the ute. He drove to where he had seen the storm damage and turned off the engine. If Jane wanted to go he didn't know how to stop her. His mother had talked of leaving, always in a nervous voice, even when it was just her and Vic alone in the house. She had told him they could just go, that there would be somewhere, somewhere far away where they would be happy. He remembered how John had said to his mother,

"I'll put you under the fuckin' ground you ever try and leave here again."

He would never say that to Jane, never think it. Yet he could not ignore that both he and John had difficult marriages. Vic had never wanted to leave, but he had wanted John gone, had prayed and begged for it. After his mother passed away John had barely spoken to him. Vic had slept in the house, and John had stayed wherever he stayed.

The morning after his mother died, John took a chainsaw and cut down fifteen she-oaks and all the grevilleas so that the house was no longer protected from the wind. That spring and summer there was no rainfall and the wind circled the house every night like a wailing Siren; doors and windows shivered in fear. A few days later John took all his mother's things—clothes, photos and even the blue curtains she had hand sewn—and burnt them. Vic remembered coming home from school to see everything ablaze and John's face, red from standing so close to the flames, sneered at him as if to say this was his idea and he no longer belonged here. To this day there was barely anything he owned that had been his mother's, apart from some Christmas decorations they made one year; and they put on the front gate every year after that. He kept them in a box in the wardrobe.

He curled down in the ute's threadbare seat, his forehead on the driver's door. The apple trees were waiting for him, but he considered, once more, his options. He could stay and try to make things work, but without irrigation it didn't make much sense. He could sell, clear the debt, and then what? Stay in Henrithvale and be the bloke that chucked it all in, the one who said he would stand alongside everyone else, and then turned around and did what was best for him. It wouldn't work. He knew he'd have to move. Jane wanted to be where there were more people, but that wasn't anything he cared for. He just couldn't see it, and the thought of being estranged from his daughters appalled him, but he also thought that maybe they'd be better off. He had always kept a deliberate space between them. It was easy to explain away; the farm had never-ending work.  It was safer for them and for him.

He recalled one of his favourite football games. He must have been ten and John was at his peak. Henrithvale were down by seven goals going into the last quarter. Vic went out on the ground to hear the coach, Jock Stewart, address the players. Jock was in the habit of belittling players with such fierceness that it took something out of them. Vic secretly wanted to hear Jock explode, but Jock circled them as if inspecting stock.

"Yer know what it is keeps a man down?" Jock asked. "It's his thinkin' he can never get up. Yer goin' to lose because that's what yer think yer should do. I can't say nothin' to yer that would do yer any good. You've got to say it to yerself, each one of yer has got to say it to himself." Then he went back to the coach's box, leaving the players standing there, stunned.

Nobody moved. It was John who gathered them all together, pulling the players into such a tight huddle that they became a single entity. Vic, standing on the outskirts with the other spectators, couldn't make out individual words but John's boorish voice was unmistakeable. The siren sounded to start the last quarter and inside twenty-five minutes Henrithvale had kicked nine goals. They won the game by twelve points. It had seemed impossible but then Vic had watched it happen. He tried to remember it in every game he played. No matter how far behind the team fell or how little he had contributed, there might be a way out. He just needed to find it.

He got out of the ute and dived into the orchard, equipped with bypass shears and a pruning saw. The trees were set out in lines, so he knew them by place, by shape and by touch. He kept notes on each one; he trusted them and they, he felt, trusted him too. He had shaped and trained them; he had helped them recover from John's tyranny as they had helped him. There were just twenty acres now of mature trees, less than half the acreage of what it had once been. Ten acres of young trees were just coming into their third year, but they were not yet making a profit.

His grandfather, an infrequent guest, worn and broken from hard work, had told him when he was twelve years old that some people are born to work the land and that it comes naturally to them. Vic was one of those people, his grandfather had said, and John was not. Vic's grandfather was not afraid of John, but he kept his distance. He came and went from Henrithvale without notice or warning until John announced one evening that he was dead. There was no funeral, just a scant burial where nobody spoke. John's mother, Vic's grandmother, had abandoned the family when John was eight. She dropped him off at school one morning and never came back. She never called and never wrote a letter. Vic found this out from Edna.

When Vic was eleven, he watched John hack away at a tree during winter pruning. His grandfather waited until John was done and had sulked away to work on another, and then he went over and rubbed his hand over the cut.

He said to Vic, "the seed of the apple doesn't turn out like the tree it came from. It becomes something of its own, sometimes better, sometimes not." Now, Vic worked with the trees until the light retreated and the air had the earthy essence of night. When he stopped his back was stiff and so were his thumbs and shoulders. He loaded the prunings into the ute and dumped them near the machinery shed, and then drove back to the house.

Jane was outside emptying the rubbish bin as he pulled into the carport. She half-smiled and he half-smiled back. He wondered if she was aware of how she had changed, if she blamed him. Maybe she thought he had cheated her, betrayed her—and likely he had.

"There was a call while you were out," Jane said as she closed the bin lid.

"Who?" he asked, but she didn't answer. She just raised her eyebrows until he understood. "Brian Hennan."

"I've just about had enough of Brian Hennan, Vic." The frustration from earlier remained. "He needs to mind his own business."

"Henrithvale is the only business he has. If he wasn't doin' that he wouldn't be doin' anything."

"Well, with any luck, soon enough he won't have anything left to worry about." She snapped. Without Henrithvale, Brian Hennan would have nothing; a captain without anyone to lead. He was unmarried, had a sister he rarely saw and agitated everybody he knew, in differing ways, with his abrupt singlemindedness. They were the only relationships he had, yet without him, Vic did not think the town would survive. Jane headed for the back door with Vic close behind.

The girls were home, sitting at the kitchen table drawing pictures of themselves and Jane shopping and playing in a park. They greeted him with their usual enthusiasm, charming the room that was awash with rosemary and roast potatoes. He put his arms around them; he loved his daughters but worried he didn't have anything necessary or useful to offer them. He had seen them born, changed their nappies, bathed their chicken pox, but they belonged to Jane. If they moved to Bendigo, they would understand that more and more for themselves.

In the morning Vic drove the girls to school. The cool air and the grey sky were discouraging. He made up for it by pretending to fall asleep when he was driving so that the girls would yell out to him to wake up. Then, acting surprised, he yawned loudly and straightened the ute, drove at walking pace, and told the girls that they were in fact going at the speed of light and it made everything seem slow. They giggled and told him he was silly, but he saw them watching him, keen for more.

He started on some stories, things he'd made up, about his time at school, when he had been in the very same rooms that were now their classrooms. He invented a teacher, old Mrs Hugebottom, who was always plotting against the students and trying to steal their lunches. She had a mouth like a rubbish bin, beady eyes and a secret dungeon under the school where she forced boys and girls to do maths for days at a time. Vic made himself and Dave the heroes of these stories. They were cunning and clever, and they would always outwit her.

When he pulled the ute into the carpark at the school, he said to the girls in a hushed but excited voice,

"I think that's her car. She's back! Be careful and don't tell her you know me." They left the ute, still giggling.

He spent the whole day in the orchard and the malaise of the conditions took away the feeling in his cheeks and made his nose run, but the rain held off. He reassured the trees with his voice, speaking to them of the prosperity to come and the bountiful sunshine that would leave them in a stupor. The dusk arrived with a low fog like an incoming tide and he went back to the house and showered. He was turning out of the driveway for The Growers' Association meeting when Jane and the girls came home. They reached out their hands to him and he took both his hands off the wheel and waved back.

When he was a boy, The Henrithvale Growers' Association would meet once a month, sometimes twice a month if there was a significant issue. John was president until his death and then Brian Hennan took over. Brian, although not a farmer himself anymore, was the only person willing to commit to the job. John had led The Growers' Association the same way he had led the football team: he was resolute, tenacious and successful. Vic was ten years old when a drought damaged crops, dropped the yield and threatened to bankrupt several farms. The government at the time talked about reducing or suspending irrigation leases to farmers in the Henrithvale area, just for a single season. John became the Growers' Association spokesperson. He was on TV, talking about how such a move would kill farming in the area forever, drive up the price of fruit and vegetables, and do nothing to help the river. There was little evidence to support any of what he said, and there were good and knowledgeable people who were saying almost the opposite. John maintained farming was the soul of the country, it was where the 'real' Australians lived and that became the dominant narrative. Later there was a push for an increase in the water allotment each farmer was receiving. John again became the public face of the idea, even though a campaign had already been underway for some time; it had even been in the papers a few years earlier. That didn't matter. All that anybody seemed to remember was that John gave them more water and a bigger crop, and that meant more money.

John's role in that campaign had been resurrected on the news when he died. The news story about John's death played like an old film reel in Vic's thoughts. It showed footage of John standing in front of the apple trees, squinting and occasionally waving his right hand in front of his face to keep the flies and dust away from his eyes. The voice-over announced:

"President of The Henrithvale Growers' Association, John Whelan, was killed early yesterday morning when his ute left the road and struck a tree near his Henrithvale home." Then there was a cut to footage of the ute, taken from a distance, squashed against a single giant gum. "Whelan is widely credited with saving farming in the Henrithvale area after his campaign to firstly preserve and then increase irrigation allotments along the Sterling River was successful."

After John's death, the football club wore black armbands every game of the next season. Brian Hennan had wanted to change the name of the stand, but the idea wasn't widely supported. Vic always felt an expectation from those who loved the football club that he would take his father's place. He hated such notions, explicit or unstated; but he loved the jumper and understood the impossibility of being someone other than John's son. When he was given his father's number to wear, he took it.

Vic could see the tree against which his father's ute had shattered. There was nothing but open ground between it and the road. Now the tree was a sentinel; a guardian.

John's funeral was one of the last times the church had been open, and it spilled over with mourners. People stood outside the church doors and trailed down the stairs. Vic remembered people saying,

"I've never seen anything like it." Brian Hennan gave the eulogy and described John as:

"A gifted athlete and a devoted husband and father." He was "someone who cared more about others than he did about himself and a person whose efforts and personal sacrifice had given the town a reputation as a rural sporting bastion with a community that was unbreakable."

Then, he told the story of how John, at sixteen, had gone down to the city and spent the preseason with Collingwood. He would no doubt have been a superstar, but he met Glenda and chose love over sporting immortality, and that was the end of that. It was a kind of truth, Vic knew. There was no mention that Glenda had been part of an end-of-season contest, during which the players put together a list of Henrithvale girls, ranking them according to their desirability, and competing to see who could seduce the greatest number. The higher a girl's rank the more points she was worth. It was a contest John had lost. He reminded Glenda of it sometimes, but she never responded.

Vic didn't speak at the funeral; Brian said that Vic was overcome with grief. The truth was that Vic didn't know what he felt, still wasn't sure, but he knew it wasn't grief.

He remembered sitting on the couch at home and hearing an indistinct sound as if giant hands were trying to conceal thunder. Soon after, Brian Hennan was knocking feverishly on the back door of the house, trying to remain composed. It was a miserable night, bordering on winter, a few weeks after Vic turned eighteen.

Vic called the police and went with Brian to the tree. He had a stinging sensation in his legs but felt no sense of urgency or horror. At the site of the accident, there was a strong stench of beer and oil that contaminated the air and leaked into his clothes. Vic was later told that the steering wheel had broken John's ribs and his jaw. Both his lungs had been punctured. Vic saw a glimpse, by torch light, of his father's face swollen and bloodied. Brian's car was parked on the shoulder of the road, but why he had been present to witness the accident, why he might have trailed John home, was never asked. Vic didn't care, not then and not now. Brian, faint and dry retching with shock had stood next to him as they waited by his car. They did not say a word at the time and never spoke of it afterwards.

Tom Walsh, the last cop Henrithvale had before the police station was closed, had been at The Growers' Association meeting with John and Brian a few hours earlier. He arrived and helped Brian clean up the beer cans that were littered around the car. He also spoke to senior investigators. The coroner later found that exhaustion had been the cause of the accident. John had been working late, as normal, in his capacity as president of The Growers' Association and had fallen asleep at the wheel while driving home. Alcohol wasn't a factor; John had a few beers, but nothing excessive. He always drank responsibly. That's why there wasn't a skid mark, why there was no attempt to swerve and miss the only tree in the paddock.

Afterwards, Vic felt an exhilarating relief; he had not only survived but prevailed. He gathered all of John's things, his clothes, football trophies, anything he could get his hands on, and burned the lot. He took his time, sat in the freezing night and watched the orange glow as it belittled John; later he buried what the flames would not take away. He thought, then, that the house was his.

— ★ —

Vic pulled into the car park of the primary school twenty minutes early, but Brian had already arrived. He would be busy setting things up in the classroom at the rear of the building, moving tables into an oval shape, arranging chairs so that his back would be against the blackboard and his eyes would always have a clear view of the door. Vic sat in the ute and felt a chill come in through the driver's side window. Another car pulled into the car park, swamping the ute with its headlights. Vic made his way to the school building, wiped his feet on the mat and pushed the door open. The room was lit by weary fluorescent bulbs that hummed and hissed to each other.

"Do feel free, Victor, to come and help out if you arrive early. It might seem as if I am having the time of my life, but I assure you, I am not." Brian was wheezing and pushed out his words between breaths, his shirt was untucked, and his tie had twisted. He grimaced as he crossed the floor as if carrying himself had become too onerous.

"You alright, Brian?" Vic asked as he helped Brian fit the last table into place.

"I'll say that I did more than I should have on Saturday, as I think you would be aware, and now I've come up sore."

Before Vic could respond a tall, square-shouldered man stomped his feet on the mat outside and entered the room. He marched purposely towards Vic and Brian. His torso, long and wide seemed out of proportion to the rest of his body; a breath tarnished with cigarettes heralded his words.

"Kenneth Moore, looking for Brian Hennan." Brian held out his hand and Kenneth shook it. Vic guessed they were around the same age.

"Good to put a face to a voice, Kenneth," Brian said.

"Ken'll do," Ken said and sized Vic up.

"Well, Ken, this is Vic Whelan, one of the growers in the area." Brian seemed nervous and he put a hand on Vic's shoulder as if he were a shy child. Ken and Vic shook hands and Brian continued talking. "Ken has come across from Sterling River to talk about the experience they had with the requisition of irrigation leases."

"Still farming in Sterling River?" Vic asked with surprise. He had heard that the town was all but gone.

"Not anymore, no. If there was, I wouldn't be here." Ken's voice was abrasive, and his words were infused with exasperation.

There was a silence as Vic considered how to continue.

"You're John Whelan's son, aren't you?" Ken demanded.

"Yeah." Vic knew what was coming. It had happened regularly in the years after John's death.

"Saw him play against Sterling River, must be more than twenty years ago, never forget it. Best bloody footballer I've ever seen. Better than those mugs on the TV."

Vic outwardly welcomed Ken's words as was expected.

Ken leaned back slightly to assess Vic.

"Don't take after him do ya?"

"No."

"Too bloody bad for you." Vic wondered how long Brian would bear profanity, or maybe he would make one of his rare concessions.

"Ken, if you would like to come and get a coffee," Brian intervened, "I can let you know what we should cover."

Brian and Ken moved down to a table near the door where Brian had set up tea, coffee, a packet of plain biscuits and some pamphlets on what membership in The Henrithvale Growers' Association could offer. The meetings had been full in recent months. There were twelve farms remaining in the area, but now local proprietors were coming along as well. Brian wanted to create a sense that the community was pulling together, a siege mentality, but Vic knew, like the rest of those who ran farms, that if the irrigation leases went, then so too did the workers and the industry that supported local business. He went outside, where the trees swayed back and forth, and sat on a tree stump near the door. The only way out of the whole dilemma, he thought, the only way to keep the farm and satisfy Jane, would be a lottery win.

Over the next half hour, the small classroom filled, with close to thirty people showing up for the evening meeting. Dave was the last to arrive; it reminded Vic of their school days. Dave had June, his wife, with him. Vic met them at the door.

"You checkin' tickets, are ya, Vic?"

"There's a dress code, Dave. It's a formal event," Vic said, as he cast a disapproving eye over Dave's ragged overalls.

"I promise not to take me dick out; is that formal enough?" Dave responded. June laughed; it was a loud horsey sounding laugh that always made people look. Dave put his arm around her waist. "Not until I get home anyway, or maybe in the car. See how things go." June rolled her eyes, but she was fond of Dave's bawdy humour and she always laughed at his jokes—jokes she must have heard over and over again; and she always laughed with genuine delight.

"Now, excuse me, ladies and gents," Brian called and people faced him. "Let's ... let's get things under way. If we can all find a seat, we can get on with what we came here for." Brian sat in the chair normally reserved for the teacher while everyone else squashed onto the student's chairs. Vic thought they looked absurd in the undersized seats, but the meetings often felt absurd so he did not mind it.

"Right, shall we?" There was no air circulation in the room, but Brian preferred it that way and would never open a window or door. Brian began as he began every meeting by sending a roll around the room so that every person in attendance could record their name.

It wasn't needed; Brian did it for his own purposes. He had been challenged on it a few times that Vic could remember but his long and passionate defence overcame any opposition. He then set up his tape recorder in the middle of the room. He still used cassette tapes, as a way of keeping minutes. Later, he would transcribe the recordings.

"Make them available to anyone who was in attendance or is a registered member of The Henrithvale Growers' Association and was unable to attend." Vic did not know of anyone who had taken up his offer.

"Now, this evening we are very fortunate to have with us, Mr Kenneth, Ken, Moore the current president of The Sterling River Growers' Association." Brian's voice conveyed a more than usual seriousness. "Right, well, I've asked Ken to come along this evening to outline exactly what happened to the irrigation leases in Sterling River and what he learned from dealing with the people who we are now dealing with."

The focus fell onto Ken, squashed onto a small chair next to Brian at the front of the room. He stood up and looked over the gathering before him as if waiting for a cue to begin.

"Put simply," Ken said as he pulled at the sides of his loose-fitting pants, "we lost the leases. Now some, those that read the writing on the wall, sold the whole kit and caboodle when they had the chance. Some tried to hang on and make a fist of it, but I tell you this for nothing, if you thought you were doin' it tough now, try doin' it without any bloody water." He spoke as if the question unnecessarily complicated events.

There was silence. Then the first question came from Rob Masterson, one of the few people in Henrithvale Vic would be glad to never see again. He was a behemoth, broad shoulders and thick legs, but his sullen face with its small features seemed misplaced. He no longer played football but kept the Henrithvale CFA branch going. He had, Vic recalled, since they were in school together, seemed in a state of constant agitation. When he spoke at meetings it was with a condescending sense of incredulity.

"So, what you're sayin', mate, is they just turn up and turn your pump off and that's it?" Rob often treated meetings as if they were part of some rich hoax, but his attendance was near perfect.

"Yes, not without warning, but yes. Now that warning was different for different people, but there came a day when that was it." He paused. "Some negotiated a reduction over eighteen months, and some signed the paperwork and off it went."

"Why?" Rob's voice was sharp.

"How the bloody hell should I know? If I could answer that I wouldn't be standin' here." Ken shot back.

"Were you aware, Ken?" Brian interrupted, "or in your opinion, was there a—a —a coercion to have people sign on the dotted line?" It was obvious Brian had rehearsed the question.

"I wouldn't call it coercion, no. I'd call it a financial incentive." Ken derided the question. "Some of the growers, no doubt like some of you here, had contracts and crop they couldn't turn their back on at the drop of a hat. They tended to be the ones who were weaned."

"How many stayed on?" Dave called out, and Ken scanned the room until he could put a face to the question.

"We had twenty-six farms in the area that sourced water from Sterling River. Twenty-two sold, which left four. Inside eighteen months they were all finished." Ken's answer sent a ripple through the group. Brian looked as if he wanted to seize control of events; he no doubt had questions to ask, questions that would give people a renewed sense of confidence in him.

"What about local business?" Etta Place, proprietor of the Royal Mail, stood up from her seat. A tall voluptuous woman, she had arrived in Henrithvale in her early twenties, purchased the Royal Mail and been its sole proprietor for nearly fifty years. She was the only person Vic could remember who refused to be impressed by John. Sometimes she would call Glenda and let her know when John was on his way home, but for the most part she kept herself at a distance. Vic had wanted, still wanted, to thank her for her phone calls. He only drank socially, just a beer or two, but Etta treated him like a stranger.

Brian interrupted:

"Before we get to these types of questions, we need to establish a sense of order. We might well be in a classroom, but—"

"Brian, I didn't ask you!" Etta scolded him.

Ken looked at Brian, then back at Etta.

"What do you think happened?" Ken asked. "The pub survived but not much else. It wasn't overnight, but one by one they went. Rural town, no industry, nothing but passing trade. That won't work."

"Any government money for that?" Etta asked.

"Not one cent." There was an uneasiness settling in. Vic tried to speak to Dave, but he was leaning over to hear something that June was saying.

"Now if we are going to avoid this sort of thing, we need to make sure we all stick together—" Brian began.

"Together?" Ken disparaged. "We had the same bloody idea, but they offer this bloke a little more than that bloke, what do you think happens? A bit more money for the first few that sign on, they'll take it."

"This is Henrithvale." Brian was angry now and he stood up. "There is mounting pressure on government to put an end to this. Now those of you who have had a read of the article in the paper will be aware that this isn't a cut and dry issue any more." Brian leaned forward and pounded his palms down onto the table. The windows in the classroom had fogged over.

"Sterling River was the first town in a long line; its experience is something we can use. It's an election year, so we need to make this an election issue."

There was already too much for people in the room to talk about, and Brian could not contain them. Ken's voice, somewhat more controlled, broke through the commotion. Brian sat down.

"I will say this: there were plenty of blokes about working to make sure deals got done."

"What does that mean?" Rob asked.

"What do you reckon it means?" Ken's hands came to rest on his hips. "It means there were blokes who came out and did all they could do to get a signature. Brian's right on the money when he says it's one in, all in. Once the first one goes that's it."

Vic could sense the division in the room. If he or any of the others decided to sell, then they sold the town as well. It was clear the requisition letters spoke of a shared fate, but now it was publicly stated. Maybe this was Brian's point.

Ken turned to Brian.

"Best of luck to you," he said and made for the door as if he had been called away.

Brian, Vic saw, was stunned. He reordered papers on his desk as conversations ignited and flourished in different parts of the room; then he tried to chase after Ken.

Dave let out a groan and stood up.

"Let's have a break, folks; give it ten minutes," he said, addressing the group. The conversations continued and people began heading towards the tea and biscuits. Dave sat down next to Vic. "Fuck me dead, what was goin' through Brian's head?"

Vic shrugged. He was glad that Jane had stayed at home. Dave nudged Vic with his forearm.

"Better keep June outta mischief," he said and made his way to the tea and biscuits. Ten minutes later Brian called people back to order and stood at the front of the room.

"Look, I think I should explain something here," he said, seemingly addressing his own confusion. "I asked Ken to come along tonight so we could see where Sterling River went wrong. Now that is a bit unsavoury, I know, and I beg your pardon if some of you felt put out by it." People were listening but Vic could see how vulnerable they were, it was in their eyes, in their posture and the way their hands fidgeted. "Henrithvale and Sterling River are not the same—not by a long shot."

"Brian, what do ya actually know?" It was Rob again. "Tell me somethin' useful will ya?"

"This is what I know, Robert: that in an election year, of all years, under significant pressure, from opposition and the wider public, a sitting government will not, will not," he thrust the words at Rob as he brushed his thinning hair away from his forehead, "move on a contentious issue. Now if we—"

"You in government now, Brian? You're talkin' outta ya arse. This is bullshit!" Rob's eyes were fixed on Brian and he pushed up the sleeves of his shirt on both arms.

"Shut up and listen, will ya," Dave interjected. He and Rob had never found common ground.

"Are you his keeper, Foster?"

"Now listen to me, both of you." Brian spoke firmly. The room was oppressively stuffy; Vic could see the condensation sliding down the drab windows to his left and right. "We will have civility in these meetings as long as I am Chair. I might be the wrong side of seventy but have no fear that I will put you out if this continues." Brian waited for a response but none came. Then he leant forward and continued. "Right, know this, Robert and David in particular, if we stick together, one behind the other then we can make it all too hard for the requisition of water leases or anything else. That is what we all need to do."

Vic, half-heartedly, put up his hand and Brian pointed at him.

"You reckon if we wait long enough they'll just go away, it won't be worth the fight?" It gave Brian the focus Vic knew he needed.

"Simply put, Vic, but yes. It's not always the best approach but it's the best approach right now for Henrithvale. We've got to make it too hard for them." Vic could sense the angst in the squeaking of chairs. It seemed an insipid plan. Brian let the silence exhaust the room.

"Before we get into administrative matters, I am going to offer some wise advice. I have spoken to Ken on the telephone at length during the past months and I want to touch on something he mentioned here tonight. There will be people in the area who will want you to sell and they will no doubt grease palms." His eyes found their way to Vic and stayed there. Vic was certain now that Brian doubted him. "Well, I won't say anything more, only there is a right way and a wrong way to deal with these people."

Brian waited again but nobody spoke. Vic's eyes fell to the burgundy carpet that had been dirtied by his boots.

The meeting moved through administrative matters and fee arrears. When Brian closed the meeting, Vic helped him stack the chairs and move the tables back into position for the morning classes. Maybe Mulholland had been to other farms. Maybe he was trying to widen the divide by nurturing doubt.

"It was nice to see June come along this evening," Brian said, as he packed the refreshments into a box and Vic unplugged the kettle. "It sends the right message about an appropriate response not only from a grower but from those around him." He knows, Vic thought. Maybe Jane had said something or maybe it was Mulholland.

"You know, Vic, I remember your mother. She was, let me add, a woman for whom I had the utmost respect. I remember her support for John in his capacity as captain of the football club and president of The Growers' Association." What Brian meant, Vic knew, was that he liked the way his mother kept her mouth shut, never rocked the boat. Never told anyone.

Brian took off his glasses and rubbed his eyes. Then he collected his things.

"We need a few more types like that around."

Brian, Vic thought, didn't know anything about his mother. Vic remembered his mother getting weak and going into hospital, coming home, going back to hospital. Mostly he remembered the urgency he felt for it to be over, for her to be well. No one said anything about dying. Even in the last few days, when she was confined to bed and a regional nurse stopped by twice per day, Vic had believed that she would be alright. He had a preference for disbelief over catastrophe, just like her.

Vic was on his way home from school, riding a rusty bike on the rough edges of the road, when Constable Tom Walsh had stopped him to tell him that his mother had died.

"I went to the school, Vic, but you'd already left. People are looking for you."

Tom reached out a hand and took a firm grip of Vic's shoulder. He went on talking but all Vic heard was the wind. He had lost something unnameable, something he knew was intrinsic to who he was, something that could not be recovered.

Tom, standing next to Vic on the roadside, put his other hand on Vic's other shoulder, and said something about his own mother. Then he put Vic's bike in the boot and drove him home. There were a dozen cars parked outside the house. Vic opened the door of the cop car and started running. He ran for the railway cutting, feeling panicked and wild. Finding the tracks, he fell to the ground and vomited, crying uncontrollably.

It was Dave Foster who found him. Dave sat next to Vic and cried too, and then he put his arms around Vic, letting Vic rest his head on his shoulder. It wasn't the first time. When John had an episode, when he pushed Vic out of the house, when he turned on Glenda, this was the place where Vic would come. He often went to the desperadoes and would be urged to bring an everlasting end to matters with "ol' John." In those younger years, Dave would put his arms around Vic, hugging him like his own mother would and Vic would find comfort in it.

The day of his mother's death, after Vic had cried himself to near breakdown, when he and Dave were close, their mouths had pressed together. Their fingers locked and held. Neither he nor Dave had acted; it was the combination of events that had brought things about. It was also the end of the intimacy they had shared and the start of something uncomfortable but also more certain, more predictable.

When he got back to the house, Brian Hennan caught him before he came in the door and pulled him out to the carport by the back of his shirt.

"Something you need to understand here," he said, pushing Vic up against his father's ute. "You've lost a mother, but that man in there, your father, he has lost a wife—and you've gone off to blazes. Get in there and give the man some support. Your family, this town, we stick together. Neighbour helps neighbour."

– ★ –

Vic finished stacking the chairs and mumbled something to Brian about needing to get home. He hurried outside to the ute, his mother's funeral paralysing him; he would never forget the spoiled air in the church and the petrified perfume of fresh cut flowers. People were there, Vic knew, for John. Dave sat near Vic in the church, but they didn't make eye contact. Herbert and Edna spoke to him at the wake, told him she was a much better woman than John had any right to marry, told him that if he needed anything he just needed to stop by the store.

As he drove home from the meeting, Vic thought about his mother buried in the cemetery, next to John, with a view by day of curved hills and, by night, of sky punctured by millions of stars. The farm, he thought, was her place too, but John would not let her be. Vic had never told anyone—not even Jane—but he thought that dying was the nicest thing John had ever done for him. He only wished he had done it sooner, when his mother was still alive. Yet the old man remained and Vic could not separate her from him. Her death gave John a permanent ownership. He decided where she should be buried, and she became John's dead wife, the sympathy was all for him. Vic wondered what they could've had, him and his mum, if John had gone first. No, John still had her and try as he did, Vic could not wrestle her away.

The windows in the kitchen were dirty and the view outside was obscured by a thin layer of dust hardened onto the glass by the heat of summer. Still, Vic saw the smoke drifting across the sky. It was subtle, blending into the grey of the flat clouds, but he recognised it straight away.

He had woken up early, before Jane and the girls, and had been eating breakfast, trying to figure out what kind of day it would be, and there it was, the smoke from the station house. He put down his coffee, there was no time to finish it, left a half-eaten piece of toast on the plate and put on his coat as he left the house in a flurry. He drove the ute to the far end of the orchard; then made his way on foot in a clumsy run over the top paddock to the railway cutting.

In the cutting, native ferns were being overrun by serrated tussock that had colonised the area. The frosty mornings had faded the tussocks, they appeared brittle but still made for hard going. Increasingly, there was something wrong with the air. His mouth was filling with saliva, but his lips were too numb to spit. There was a feeling in his legs like he had pissed himself. Fear got its nails under his clothes and dragged them over his skin; he paused at the edge of the cutting, just before it dipped and straightened out to the station house. Slender thistles, those that had flowered last season and those on the cusp of flowering, gathered in bands and their barbed seeds grasped at his legs as he waded through them. The station house came into view as an arctic gust blocked his way. He put his shoulder to it and kept moving.

There was something different, something he hadn't seen before. The lean desperado was sitting outside the station house on the platform, perched on a chair that was tilted back on two legs. He cradled a rifle across his knees, and hadn't seemed to notice Vic; indeed, he made no movement at all until Vic was near the top of the stairs that led onto the platform. Then the lean desperado adjusted his weight so the chair silently dropped back onto its four legs. With his left hand he combed down his moustache. Vic faltered.

"I seen you comin' in." The desperado spoke without looking at Vic. "Thought about sendin' one your way," he tapped the rifle with his right hand, "keep you on your toes." Vic sat down on the platform next to the desperado, the rough sandstone bricks of the station house pressed against his coat. "I'd invite you to take a chair, but the old boy in there," he gestured to the station house with a flick of his head, "he ain't in the mood. Best not to agitate him."

Vic and the desperado took in the vast hills of yellowing grass that wilted with the remnants of summer heat. They were surrounded by open fields and nothing, no one to tell them what to do. They sat this way for a long time and the only thing Vic heard was the meditative exhale of the breeze. He had almost fallen asleep when he felt the desperado's eyes.

"You done somethin' 'bout that ranch of yours yet?" His left hand cocked the rifle, and he studied the horizon. He let the rifle sit cocked across his lap and Vic longed to reach out and take it for his own.

"I don't know what there is to be done." Sometimes Vic felt himself mimicking the desperado's voice, felt his own words sounding as if they were shaped by the desperado's mouth.

"Well, so be it." The desperado stood up, saw something in the distance and his stance became rigid. He lifted the rifle, pushed the hilt into his shoulder and leaned his head to one side so that he could see straight down the barrel. His finger rested lightly on the trigger. Then, just as suddenly he turned and stood over Vic.

"You reach your decision damn quicker 'an most would."

"Jane doesn't want to stay, and without irrigation I can't grow a damn thing. And the school?" Vic felt as if the desperado might turn and strike him with the rifle, so he remained completely still.

"Well it's all jus' done for then, ain't it?" The desperado spat and returned to his seat, uncocking the rifle that again rested on his lap, the barrel pointed away from Vic. The desperado tapped his fingers quickly on the stock. "I hear you sayin' it, but I don't see nothin' to the doin'. Sayin' it is somethin', but doin' it is somethin' else all different."

Vic didn't know what to say. There was a letter at home, which gave him the option on settlement, anywhere from thirty to ninety days, or by negotiation if needed. All he had to do was sign. No need for lawyers or conveyance; that would all be taken care of. It would be easy.

"Yeah well, there you go," Vic stood up. His back ached and he rubbed at it with his hands.

"Here it is as I see it." The desperado eased back into his chair. "I knew a man took a fox cub, tried ta raise it up like a dog, kept it tied ta his house. After a time, it stopped eatin', starved itself. Man said it was nothin' but a dumb animal. That fox jus' knew what livin' was and what it ain't." The desperado took in a breath, so his nostrils flared, then closed his eyes.

Vic knew that it was time to leave, just as he had always known when it was time to come here. He crept away, taking the stairs carefully, but once he felt the ground underfoot he started to run. The vast hills were gone and now the ground was rough. Thistles scratched his hands but he kept running, only stopping once he was inside the cutting.

He had told Dave about the station house when they were boys and had invited him to see it, but his conviction broke the make-believe and Dave declined. The next time Vic saw the smoke the lean desperado met him at the door, snarling:

"It ain't no event for one an' all." Then he slammed the door shut and Vic didn't see him again for months.

Vic could hear the wind as he climbed out of the cutting, his flared nostrils searching for air; he slipped as he tried to gain his footing, stood up and wiped his muddy hands on his pants. Then he crossed the undulating, windswept land as a bulbous storm bullied its way through the valley making the morning seem like evening.

Vic ate the rest of his toast and gazed down into the lukewarm cup of coffee. He heard Jane close the bedroom door, heard the groan of the weak floorboards as she approached. She hesitated before she came into the kitchen.

"Morning, Vic, how was the meeting?" She crossed to the bench and turned on the kettle. He wondered if she cared or if she was just looking for another fracture.

"Rob got a bit fired up." He surprised by how many spoons of instant coffee she heaped into her cup.

"What about?" She sat down at the kitchen table directly across from him. Maybe this was a peace talk.

"Kenneth, Ken Moore. He was the president of The Sterling River Growers' Association. I guess he still is." Vic took a sip from the cup and flinched at its unpleasantness. "Most of the farms in Sterling

River took the government deal and those that didn't ended up in the shit," he spat sharp words at her, then pushed his palms flat against the table. She was surprised at him. He had never said an angry word to her, never raised his voice to anyone, except on a football field; and he saw an ugliness in his words that tied him to the past.

"Sorry...sorry," he apologised.

"Ah, Vic." She sounded worried.

"I dunno, Jane. I just dunno." He spat out a breath. "What a fuckin' mess it is."

They'd been happy for a long time. It had been too easily forgotten. He wanted her to fight with him to keep the farm, to save his mother; so that even if they lost everything, he would still belong to somewhere, to someone. The candidness that endeared them to each other had been too cheaply sold.

"It's hard, Vic, I know it is."

"Yeah." He scratched at the sides of his head, rocked forward and leaned against the table."

"It just won't work to wait it out this time. Don't you think?"

"What then?"

Sarah and Emily came into the kitchen, dressed for school. Jane got up and left the table.

"I'm taking the girls to school, then I'm meeting mum half-way." Half-way was between Henrithvale and Bendigo. They would both drive the ninety or so minutes to a half-way point, meeting at a truck stop next to a McDonald's.

"I can take the girls," Vic offered in a contrite voice.

"No, it's on the way. I'll get them on my way home."

"Have a good day, girls." They rushed over to where he was seated at the table, their eyes brightening up to the sound of his voice. He wanted to impart some lesson or advice that would make them happy and safe. He reached out his hands to them.

"Remember, if you get everything right, ya might not have to go back."

They thrilled, as they always did, in his jokes and comments. He stood up and kissed them both on the forehead and then clumsily kissed Jane; she gave him a sympathetic look and guided the girls out the back door.

Vic pushed aside the coffee and thought of his father. There had been a time when Vic was younger, maybe eight or nine, when John would take him to footy training and sometimes to The Growers' Association meetings. It was an initiation most boys in the area went through, and it provided the beginning of what became lifelong routines.

There was something in Vic that John didn't like. There was something he wanted to fix and, in the end, when he couldn't fix it, he kept away from it. Vic knew when it had started, when John had first recognised it. They were at football training for the under-tens on a Tuesday after school and John had come down early to talk with the other fathers. There was a practice match going on and try as he would Vic could not get near the ball, could not do the things as the other kids did them. Still, he had enjoyed the game, but after training he ran over to John and the other fathers grouped in front of the stand. Someone said,

"Vic, get your old man to show you how to kick."

"And run," added another.

There were sniggers and snorts from John's friends, but John didn't like it. Vic knew right away. For the next few months John would kick the football with him most nights after school on the patchy lawn behind the house. John told him he needed to get his head over the ball and kick through it, not jab. There was reserved praise when Vic did something John approved of and irritated noises when he did not. Vic had the sense then, still did at times, that if he could please John, be someone John wanted him to be, then John would not punish Glenda for his failings.

Some nights when John was late home, Vic would wait for him out on the lawn, kicking the ball to himself. He would kick the football in the air, catch it and run off, doing the same thing over and over again. While he did this, he would call out what was happening, commentating on some game that was taking place inside his head. It was a game in which he was the star and there was a Grand Final to be won, and he was the player to kick the winning goal for Henrithvale. When he got home, John would tell him to cut it out, but Vic couldn't help it. The last time it happened Vic felt John's chapped hand jerk him backwards and out of the final seconds of another game he was about to win.

"Enough of this shit," John growled.

With his other hand John snatched the football out of Vic's arms.

"You can have this back when ya know what it's for." Then John and the football were gone. After that John went to footy training alone and told Vic he had to stay home when The Growers' Association meetings were on. They were school nights after all.

Vic cried as he always did and stood there puzzled as to what to do.

His mother had been watching through the kitchen window, but waited for him to come inside before she said anything.

"It's alright mate, he doesn't mean it." Her voice always calmed him. She knelt and hugged him, her clothes perfumed by the onions she had been chopping. A week later there was a new second-hand football waiting for Vic when he came home from school. His mother told him to keep it under his bed. She said John didn't need to know everything. What he wanted, but what he knew now was unreasonable, was for her to challenge the way John treated him when it was happening. The explosive voice and barbarous words, the open-handed slaps to the side of the head for minor indiscretions did not pain him as much as her heartbroken silence. It wasn't her fault and he was no better. If she had failed him, he had failed her too.

Vic spent the morning and early afternoon tending to the orchard. He couldn't prune with the type of gloves that protected his hands from the wintry sting, couldn't grip the sheers or the saw, and had to bear the dazing soreness that came with the conditions. His hands felt as if they were broken; occasionally a blustery rain would break through the melancholy, torment him and then retreat, only to return. The trees were bare, nothing but bony limbs reaching to the sky for alms. Yet at the centre of the orchard there were twelve orphic trees, Black Twigs his grandfather called them, each more than a century old; vestiges of a past orchard. These trees never seemed to be without large, scarlet fruit. Vic had tried and failed many times to grow something from their seeds. Even John had left them alone. Their constant abundance seemed to admonish the rest of the orchard.

The Black Twigs were in a rough circle and the centre of this circle was thought to be the place where Vic's great-great uncle Warren was buried, although there was also a gravestone for him in the old section of the Henrithvale cemetery. Vic's grandfather said that Warren had been buried in the centre of the orchard after he drowned in the flooded Sterling River. An empty coffin was buried in the cemetery to appease the church. Vic recalled his grandfather at rest in the grove, calling himself Lazy Lawrence. Sometimes Vic found himself in earnest conversation with these trees about his mother, Jane and his daughters. But he had not mentioned the requisition of the irrigation leases and he wondered if the trees knew, if they understood.

Late afternoon came with an encircling hail. Vic packed up for the day and sat in the ute drinking coffee from a thermos. When there was no letup, he changed into dry clothes and took the ute into town to see Herbert and Edna. The general store was closed again, but its door was open. Inside there was an empty ice-cream container so that people could pay for their papers, although there were no papers to be seen and the container was empty. The room was uninviting as if no one had been in there for years. Vic made his way behind the counter and opened the door that led into Herbert and Edna's house. He stood and listened, then heard the murmurings of a radio.

"Jack, you there?" He started down the hall and Herbert came out of the kitchen to meet him, his face partly hidden by a half-opened door.

"Here he is, the next Henrithvale premiership winner!"

"Thought I'd drop in, see how things are."

"Come and have a cuppa."

Vic sat down at the kitchen table and Herbert went about making a sandwich. It seemed to Vic that nothing much had changed here in all the time he had known Herbert and Edna, although the strong growth of the rhododendron bush outside the kitchen window shaped light in the room differently each year.

Herbert put the sandwich aside and rested the palms of his hands against the edge of the bench. He seemed about to speak, and then stopped. His head started to droop and he began sobbing. Vic wavered and then moved towards Herbert as if he might embrace him, but stopped himself an arm's length away. He put a hand on Herbert's shoulder. Herbert steadied himself, then reached up and patted Vic's hand so that Vic took it away.

"Bloody hard this thing is, Vic." He turned and rubbed at the rims of his eyes. "Girls are coming up to help out." Herbert and Edna's daughters were several years older than Vic; they had moved away as soon as they had finished high school, visiting irregularly.

"I'm sorry, Jack." Vic couldn't say more. He still wasn't convinced that Edna would die, but then, he thought, he had never believed that his mother would either.

"The girls want to move us down to the city. A care place that deals with this sort of thing." Herbert, Vic thought, had given in to pressure. "She says she doesn't need it, but I reckon we'll go, just for a bit."

"I'll keep an eye on things for ya." Vic said. "I'll try not to steal too much." He hoped he might lift Herbert's mood.

Herbert sighed a smile of appreciation, turned back to the bench and switched the kettle on. Vic took two cups out of a corner cupboard and Herbert placed a tea bag in each one.

"Got some biscuits here somewhere," Herbert said as he opened cupboards.

"Next to the sink, on your right," Vic remembered. Herbert opened the cupboard and there they were.

"You'll have to move in, Vic." Edna's raspy voice surprised him from the doorway that led into the kitchen. Herbert panicked and rushed over to support her.

"It's alright, Jack, I'm not an invalid just yet." Nevertheless, she let Herbert help her to a seat, and Vic made an extra cup of tea. The three of them sat around the table.

"Girls coming up, Jack was saying." Vic sipped the hot tea.

"So they say, but I've heard that before." Edna's cup was a great weight for her unsteady hands.

"How was the meeting?" Herbert asked after a long silence.

"Aw, yes, those bloody meetings," Edna added, "and that tape recorder." she sneered.

"Yeah, was alright. Nothin's changed."

"Well, there you are. Don't sit around waiting anymore." Vic saw how emaciated her face had become, and that her eyes had milky film over them. "Jane's a lovely girl, but she's not the sort to stay here, not with what's happening." Vic stared at the cup of tea in his hands, turning it around and around.

"Grand Final on Saturday. Brian must be beside himself?" Herbert asked before Edna could say anymore.

"Played it pretty close to his chest so far," Vic said, keeping his eyes on the heat rising from the cup.

Edna watched them, then put her cup down.

"You can talk football all you like, but something will happen whether you want it to or not." There was a rattle in her lungs when she spoke

"I'm just waitin' on a few things, Ed. Isn't much to say."

"Not to me there isn't, you say it to her..." Edna's voice fell into to a cough: a broken sound that came from her lungs. Herbert braced her.

Vic wanted to leave. He got up and put his right hand lightly on Edna's shoulder as the coughing fit subsided, then shook hands with Herbert.

In those days after his mother had passed away, he remembered seeing his reflection in a mirror and thinking how strange he was, how remote. That was how Herbert looked now. Vic had no words for him. He put his cup, still mostly full, in the sink and made his way back to the ute. He sat there a minute, bathing in the icy air that had leaked into the cabin, feeling like he needed to wash something off his skin.

— ★ —

It had taken more than a decade after John's death for Vic to reclaim the orchard from his father's failures and foolishness. In all that time there was never a profit, but each season accumulated a little less debt than the season before. There was no time for complacency, and every season seemed to bring a codling moth plague no matter how much work he did to remove their overwintering sites. He had spent the last autumn banking earth against the trees, just him and a shovel. The stink of the mint and honey eucalyptus balm Jane rubbed into his lower back every night would forever remind him of blistered palms and mud-clogged boots— and Jane's hands.

Maybe, without him, a few trees would hold on, but in time everything would go. Perhaps, fifty or sixty years from now, Sarah or Emily would take their grandchildren out this way, if the river hadn't been dammed. With vague and failing memories, they would point to where they thought the house had been and where the trees might have been. But they would know nothing of his mother— only of John, who they would find celebrated in a hundred newspaper clippings that spoke of his achievements on the football field and with the Growers' Association. Vic could not deny these achievements and that they gave life to the community, and he wanted so dearly to replicate them on the football field, but they were unjust accolades. Perhaps the girls would visit the cemetery, but they would never know the truth of it. His mother would only ever be an image in a few sun-worn photographs.

The rain was gone and there was barely any light left in the day as Vic wandered among the trees. Maybe he should let them know. It was their fate too. Then he heard someone whistling, but he couldn't tell from which direction it was coming. The wind carried it and turned it over. Vic went further into the orchard and crouched down so the branches didn't obscure his view; down low the bitterness of the day found its way in through his clothes. He moved into the centre of the orchard, so he felt submerged and hidden and safe. The banking he had done in the autumn made the ground between the trees soft and his boots squelched and stuck with each step. The wind suddenly dropped and there was nothing but the shrill squawk of cockatoos and then silence.

He stood up and heard the whistling again, louder, closer. It was behind him. He turned around to catch sight of someone moving amongst the Black Twigs, not thirty metres away; he took off his boots and socks and ran barefoot, ducking under some branches to find William Mulholland.

Mulholland didn't seem to see Vic until he was right in front of him. Then he stopped whistling.

"Ah, Vic, you've given me a start," he said as he put his left hand to his chest. "I came to speak with you but—"

"This is private property, mate. Ya can't just—" Vic could hear the wind circling around the trees.

"Oh certainly it is, Vic, and I meant no offence. I stopped by the house but there was no one to be found." Mulholland's eyes were grey whirlpools. "I caught the faintest whiff of apples on the breeze and just followed my nose." He beamed at Vic, then an apple that hung from a Black Twig branch just above his head caught his attention. "It must be marvellous to grow such beautiful things; to work with your own hands to nurture something so delicate." He waited for Vic to look at the apple. "I've great admiration for you, Vic."

"What do ya want?" Vic felt the mud, like boneless fingers, work its way between his toes.

"Want? Oh, only to talk. To be honest with you I don't mind it that folk in Henrithvale are unwilling to sell. It's a beautiful place." He reached up and cradled the apple in his hand. "Do you mind? Can you spare one?"

"S'pose." Vic put his hands in his pockets and then took them out again.

Mulholland plucked the apple from the tree and pushed it up under his nose. He closed his eyes and inhaled as if the apple were a charmed elixir, then put it in his pocket.

"You know, when I was young an apple was a rare thing, a real treat. An orchard like this would have been heaven to me as a child." He seemed to want Vic to speak, but Vic had nothing to say. "Your girls, let me think, Emily and Sarah, is it?"

"Yeah, that's it." Vic shuffled backwards so the arms of the trees rested on his shoulders.

"They must adore this place." Vic would have been glad if they had shown even a passing interest. They were young, but he knew they would not be farmers. Maybe if there had been a son, but he was glad there hadn't been and wouldn't be.

"What are ya sellin,' Mr. Mulholland?" Vic's chest tightened.

"Selling? Oh, I'm not selling anything, Vic. I'm buying is what I'm doing." He came closer to Vic, pulled the apple out of his pocket and rubbed it against the lapel of his grey suit. The wind nudged in through the trees, sending Black Twig leaves into the air. Vic wanted to find his boots. "What do you say, Vic, it's time we had a chat?"

"I don't know who the bloody hell you think you are, but I suggest—" There was something about William Mulholland, a sinisterness that told Vic to be wary.

"It's a difficult time for you, Vic, a difficult time for the whole town. One misfortune after another, isn't it? The farm, the school, everything those previous generations built." Mulholland's vigour startled Vic, "Believe me, I know what you are going through, but stubbornness in the face of calamity has no reward. Your friends, the people in town, they speak very highly of you—"

"I'm not lookin' to sell and I reckon you've had your say." Vic reminded himself of Brian, but he felt as if he were trapped in wild ocean currents. The furrows on Mulholland's brow doubled and his eyes spoke of malevolence.

"Okay, Vic. Okay. No harm done. I'll see myself away." He put the apple away and turned, the wind catching briefly inside his jacket and upsetting the collars of his shirt. He adjusted them to his satisfaction, and then turned back to Vic.

"There is just one pressing matter Vic. Do you mind?" He sounded concerned, sincere. "I've been doing this a long time." He paused. "Each time, when pressed, people will say they are connected to their home, to all those generations that have come before. They'll say that selling does these people a disservice. Is that what you think, Vic?" Vic wanted to tell Mulholland it wasn't true, but there was something beguiling in the sound of his voice.

"S'pose."

"Sentimental are you, Vic?" Vic squirmed and although he did not speak, he knew he had given himself away. "Sentimentality binds you to the past, but it also keeps you just where you are." Vic felt as if he were being dissected. "Sentimentality is like religion and it demands a spiritual sufferance. It comes from frightened people." Mulholland's eyes had a watery lustre. He seemed as if he were remembering something wonderful and his voice became very tender.

"Those things, Vic, they're not real." He put his right hand on Vic's shoulder. "Don't be a fool, Vic. Sell your farm, take the money and go live somewhere else."

The wind continued to circle around them and Vic could feel the branches pressing into his back.

"Just think about it," Mulholland hissed, removing his hand from Vic's shoulder. Then he turned and wandered back into the orchard, heading towards the house.

Vic, his feet sank into the mud, did not feel he could go after him and did not want to. Now the trees would know; and he could not, as much as he wanted to, take them with him. To abandon through choice or misfortune did not matter. Regardless of the catalyst, a wound was a wound. His mother did not die to rebuke him, to renounce him, he would not say that she did; but she did. And now the thought that he might now do the same to her, to the trees, felt like an utter catastrophe.

Vic parked the ute next to the stand that was partly illuminated by lights from the tall poles spaced around the ground's perimeter; hordes of insects were charmed by the lights, as if they offered some greater meaning to life. They weren't much really, only the centre square was useable, but before they arrived it often meant training in the change rooms. He relaxed and could see Brian as he placed witches hats out on the oval. Vic let his thoughts focus on the game to come. It would be cathartic but also revealing and he would see himself for who he truly was; and who that might be could confirm or refute truths which had carried him through his football life.

Vic took his football bag from behind the seat and made his way towards the clubrooms. In the clubrooms he found himself alone with the picture of John high on the wall. There were other photos, of premiership teams, of the oval before the stand was erected, but the photo of John was the largest. John was in his mid-twenties with a mess of black hair that reached down to his shoulders. Underneath the photo was a plaque added years later, no doubt Brian's work, that proclaimed John's achievements.

Vic started to get changed and thought of how Brian had asked many years ago if Vic would donate John's trophies and awards to the football club, so that they could be put on permanent display. Vic had told him he didn't know where they were. In the fire the plastic on the trophies had melted and bubbled giving the flames a green tinge.

Brian came into the rooms as Vic was lacing his boots.

"I need not remind you, do I, Vic, that I am not a man of your age and dexterity." Brian's face had a rosy hue and perspiration gleamed on his forehead and cheeks.

"Uh, no. I—"

"No is right. So, might I prevail upon you to provide some assistance?"

"Sorry, Brian, thought you were finished."

"Thought has nothing to do with it. Thought and Asked live at opposite ends of the street, and I can tell you this for nothing, Asked gets a lot more done than Thought." With that Brian left the clubrooms.

Vic trudged after him. Out in the night, in shorts and a worn University Blues guernsey, he felt the stiffness in his knees and hips and lower-back. He selected a footy from a basket near the fence and caressed its leather skin, then began running laps along the dark outskirts of the oval; bouncing the ball as he went. He focussed on his breathing, making sure that he bounced the ball only when he exhaled. In the sombreness, the stand seemed like a tomb from a lost civilisation. He heard a story that when it was built there were bones in the ground; kid bones, broken skulls. They were shovelled back in, buried under the foundations. When the water pipes rumbled people would sometimes make jokes about restless spirits. He ran slowly, caught occasionally in the headlights from other cars, as they made their way down to the ground and parked near the ute.

He was fifteen when he fully realised, fully accepted, that there were others, like Dave, who were better than him. A little while later he realised that they had always been better than him, but he did not see it earlier because he did not want to see it. Then the idea of it, of him, Victor Whelan, being a professional footballer became foolish. He did not think he would ever please John and it was such a despairing thought. It made the past irreparable and unchangeable. But to hand in his boots, would give truth to John's contempt and belittlement. Vic played on because he loved the game and because and in spite of his own trepidations, he wanted to be better. There were periods when he was engulfed by those inadequacies that had incensed John. It meant in some games he stayed away from the ball. Yet the thought of quitting footy and doing something else never lasted. Instead there was an urgency to be here, to always come back, with every season offering the chance for some sort of redemption. As he jogged his fifth lap Dave Foster ran out to join him.

"You done three laps, Vic?"

"Five," he said, as he exhaled, expelling any lasting doubt in his thoughts.

"Brian says you only need to run three. I'll take two of yours and do one of me own."

They ran together along the boundary line, silently handballing the football back and forth. Suddenly, Dave tucked the ball under his arm and sprinted away, baulking an imaginary opponent and then drilling the goal from forty-five metres out. He turned and raised his arms in mock victory revelry.

Dave was one of those people who never needed to do very much to stay fit; he just always seemed ready to run, to fight for the ball, to be able to kick long. He never tired. Vic told him to turn around. Brian Hennan was watching from the centre of the ground, clipboard in hand, scowling his disapproval. Dave went to collect the ball he had kicked, and Vic joined the playing group; their rapid breath and strong bodies pushing away the night.

"It will be a short run, some end-to-end kicking. We'll break into forwards, backs and mids and work on structures." Brian was wearing his light blue tracksuit pants with royal blue trimming. He had a whistle around his neck. He stood in the middle of the oval and marshalled the players into three groups. They started with one ball kicked clockwise from group to group with the player who kicked the ball running to the next group. On the second rotation another ball was introduced until eight balls were in play, so that balls and bodies were in constant flow. There was no time to think, just to move and react. The movements were familiar and predictable. Vic always played better when he didn't have time to think about what it was he needed to do.

"Trust the voice of your team mates," Brian yelled. As he caught and then kicked another ball, Vic felt himself being taken away from the complications and impossibilities beyond the game. A thought began to crystallise: Those previous years would not be so desolate if they led him to where he had so longed to be, they would be the necessary price.

As the training session ended Brian had the group run a lap, with everyone pressed in tight.

"Closer!" Brian growled. "These are your team mates, know how they run, know how they move, know how they breathe, know how they think." Vic become part of the movement of perfectly synchronised bodies gliding through the night air.

"Close your eyes!" Brian demanded, "bring up the pace." Vic didn't know who was around, but it didn't matter. He imagined them transformed into some mythical beast, each man a tendon, a muscle or a bone working in unison.

— ★ —

In the clubrooms, Vic sat on the bench listening to the conversations and movement as players began to change; steam from the shower congealed the air. Brian stood in the doorway watching for something he seemed uncertain about, and then having seemingly found it he made an announcement:

"No one is to leave just yet; there are matters, urgent matters may I add, that need to be discussed." Vic and the others casually acknowledged Brian. "Collect yourselves as you are able, and be ready in five minutes," he added before leaving.

"'Collect yourselves as you are able?'" Dave asked as he pulled on his pants. "What d'ya reckon that means?" Vic shrugged.

When Brian reappeared, he had changed back into the blue shirt with the short sleeves; his arms had a red tinge and were washed with goose bumps. He never changed in the clubrooms. Dave joked that there was a telephone box he used.

Brian held a letter in his left hand.

"The Henrithvale Football Club is part of the Western Football League, the governing body of which is The Greater Western Districts Football Association." Brian searched the room and his voice had an unsettling distress; the effect was utter silence. Vic could not recall such an absence of sound, but he had no thought as to what might be coming. "In my capacity as president of the Henrithvale Football Club, I received this letter." He held the letter high above his head, his hand was trembling, and it gave the impression that he was shaking it in angry defiance. "I will read it to you now."

Brian took the letter in both hands and held it a short distance away from his face. He cleared his throat and seemed lost. His eyes darted left, then right. Finally, as if winning a silent inner argument, he cleared his throat again.

"'Dear Mr Hennan. This letter serves as confirmation that the Western Football League, a subsidiary of The Greater Western Districts Football Association will cease operation at the conclusion of the current season. After careful examination the association has decided that The Western League is no longer financially viable, and its continued administration represents a very real threat to the financial stability of the association as a whole.'"

Vic, seated on the bench, slumped back against the wall of the clubrooms and pushed his right forearm against his forehead. He had a sudden memory of Constable Tom Walsh telling him his mother had died. There was confusion in the group, but Brian kept reading.

"'As you are no doubt aware, The Western League is currently made up of only four teams, the lowest number of teams in any league the association administers. It should also be noted that each of these teams is currently in arrears, with total outstanding fees currently at $12,000. Should Henrithvale decide to pay its outstanding debt it can petition the association to join an established league. The Henrithvale Football Club can also petition a club already in a league to facilitate a merger.'" Brian took one hand from the page and adjusted his glasses.

"'The Greater Western Districts Football Association notes that admittance to another league or merger with an established club is unlikely given the vast distances teams already need to travel and the lack of funds available to facilitate such a process.'" Brian let his left hand, holding the letter, fall to his side as if the weight was too much. He spoke directly at them. "I know that some of you, perhaps more than I am aware, have heard rumours or gossip regarding this matter. Well here it is."

Vic had clear memories, as a child, of waking from nightmares and being unable to move or speak, like a stunned fish hauled from the waters. This was the same and the room transformed; the way it looked, the way sound moved.

The Greater Western Districts Football Association had already closed three leagues that Vic knew about, amalgamated others, merged some teams and pushed others out. The articles in the papers blamed local councils that needed to move funds into other areas, the cost of public liability insurance, and a poorly managed Victorian Rural Ambulance Service. There had been three deaths the previous year in games that the Association oversaw: all heart attacks. In each case it had taken over an hour for an ambulance to arrive. It wasn't a good look.

"Is there an appeal process, Brian?" Doc asked as everyone else seemed struck mute. Vic found himself rubbing his forehead with the ends of his fingers.

"Yes, there is, and I can tell you an appeal was filed by me in my capacity as club president, with assistance from legal professionals, four weeks ago."

"When is that letter dated, Brian?" Vic didn't recognise his own voice. He stood up, feeling dizzy and weak. The players in front of him parted slightly so that Brian and Vic could see each other.

"June fifth," he said it quickly. A murmur of discontent rose from the group.

"That's more than two months ago." Vic spoke loudly, but he could barely hear himself, barely hear Brian. The sound of blood grinding to a stop reverberated in his ears.

"There was never any desire or attempt on my part to deceive anyone," Brian said. "I can tell you that this goes to my very core. But, at the heart of it, it is an administrative issue. In my capacity as club president I have handled the situation as best as was reasonably possible." Brian was, Vic knew, as interwoven with the club as anyone else in the room; but he'd had time to fortify against such a prospect.

"The appeal process, Brian?" Doc reiterated.

Vic sat down on the bench and nursed his forehead in his palms; Brian's far-off voice an inescapable torment. Something was leaving, something he did not recognise or understand, but its leaving was terrifying. In its place was a chasm. The room flipped. He tried to stand but fell sideways.

When Vic woke up there was something odd about the space he was in. The sheets were different, stiff and uncomfortable. Jane was sitting next to the bed and Dave was beside her. When he opened his eyes, Jane stood up and started calling for someone. Her voice sounded hollow and unnatural. Dave leant over him, his eyes red from lack of sleep.

"You're in the hospital mate. Just tell 'em ya fine. Tell 'em you remember everything. Tell 'em you fainted. Fainted." He spoke as if he were letting Vic in on a secret. "You scared the shit out of Jane and the kids."

Dave moved back as two nurses came in. Working together they took his blood pressure, shone a light in his eyes and asked him what his name was, what day it was, when he was married and the names of his kids. They asked him if he was under any stress, any more than usual. He said he was fine. They told him he had suffered a concussion at football training when he fell over in the clubrooms and Dave had driven him to the hospital in Bendigo. He said he remembered it all and Dave sat next to him agreeing with and supporting every answer Vic gave.

They kept him overnight for observation and let him go home the next morning. It was a difficult drive in Jane's car. Vic didn't like being a passenger, never had. He rested for the first half hour.

"Where are the girls?" He questioned.

"You've asked me that twice now. They're at school. Dave's sorting it out." Dave and June didn't have kids of their own. June couldn't.

"The girls are very worried about you," Jane said.

"I'll be alright," he muttered.

"They love their Dad, love having him around." She waited. He focussed on the road ahead. "They've been asking me if we're going to move."

He turned his head to look at her.

"What gave 'em that idea?"

"Kids talk, you know that. They're at school with kids whose families are in the same boat as us. They know their school might close. You think they don't worry?" He didn't want to answer.

"What did you tell 'em?"

Her hands gripped at the steering wheel.

"I thought that the answer would be yes." She waited. "I told them Daddy wasn't sure."

"Thanks." He leaned back in the seat, took a yawning breath; outside the passenger window he saw tawny fields and curled hills. His head was pounding. The hospital had given him the all-clear. He'd had a CAT scan, and then another after they injected him with dye. Unnecessary drama he thought. They told him no football games for a few weeks. What a joke. His legs could be broken and he'd still drag himself out on the field.

"Really?" She asked. "Poor Vic, he's the only one!" She was mad.

"What would I do then? We sell, what do I do?" His eyes stayed on the paddocks outside his window.

"Well, Vic." Jane wound up. "Maybe you could start by asking, 'what will we do? What will Jane and Emily and Sarah do? What will your family do?'"

"You'll move, be a nurse, and the girls'll go to some bigger school."

"It's not a punishment, Vic."

"I'm the one—" His voice sounded ugly and he stopped himself.

"The one what? The one what, Vic?" She demanded. "I'm the one that takes care of the girls, gets them to school and makes sure they are clothed and fed. I'm the one that makes sure the bills are paid on time. I'm the one—" Her hands held even tighter to the steering wheel. Raindrops gathered on the windscreen.

He wanted to leave, to open the door and go.

"Jane, what do ya want me to say?" She didn't get it, didn't want to understand. "No worries, we'll just sell up and off we'll go? It's just a farm, just a town. Nothin' special there." His voice grew unwillingly louder as he spoke.

"That's it, Vic, isn't it?" She shouted back. "Your farm, your town, your fucking football club are worth more than your family!" She started to cry.

He hated tears. He reached out a hand, almost withdrew it, and then rubbed her shoulder but she shrugged it away and switched on the radio; there was a sudden and abusive mix of static of electric guitars.

The car stopped before an old bridge. There were road works ahead and traffic going both ways had to share a single lane. Out his window Vic could see what remained of the Sterling River. Despite the near continuous rainfall of the last few months, it had not recovered. He remembered how high it had once been, how wide and how strong it had been; now it suffered the incurable condition of people and progress, the complacency of political rhetoric.

Vic put the seat back and shut his eyes. Jane turned off the radio and pushed her foot down on the accelerator and the car sped on. Vic dozed and thought of the first game he had ever played at a senior level for Henrithvale. They had won by four points: Vic had barely had a touch all day. They were two points down late in the last quarter, and there was that pleading with time and with the final siren to wait just a little longer. Three times the ball neared the Henrithvale goals and three times the defence swept it away. Then, when the ball was seventy metres out, Dave let go with a torpedo punt that covered sixty metres, hit the ground, bounced sharply to the left, then the right, avoided two defenders and went through for a goal; then the siren went. Vic was ready for them to lose; he had resigned himself to it. Sometimes when the memory of the game returned, he still felt they could somehow lose.

They were close to home before Vic opened his eyes. As Jane turned into their driveway Vic adjusted his seat. It was then he saw the lean desperado in the field near the front of the house. He was alone, watching Vic from under the brim of his hat. Vic stifled a gasp.

As the car passed the desperado, he stuck out his chin and spat tobacco onto the ground. What was he doing here? He had never come to Vic, it had always been Vic going to him, needing him.

"Vic? You alright?" Jane was concerned.

Overhead Vic heard the faraway roll of thunder, but when the car stopped the desperado was nowhere to be seen. Jane opened his door for him, offered him her arm to steady himself and although he didn't need it, he gladly accepted.

— ★ —

Vic's head had an irritating ache that stayed with him through the morning. To get out of the house, he moved the ute into the open-faced machinery shed and then set to cleaning it. The storm was boisterous and tugged at the corners of the shed's corrugated-iron walls, but Vic ignored it. He pulled the broken toolbox out from behind the passenger seat and sprinkled tools over the worn concrete floor. There was a plumber's wrench, wrapped in what was left of a T-shirt he had worn thirty years ago.

Vic's mother had given him the T-shirt on a vacation to Queensland. It had been John's idea to go, an unexpected and out of character decision that was silently celebrated. John did all the driving. His mother had the passenger window open, so the wind pushed back her hair, and Vic had the backseat to himself.

They drove up through New South Wales, barely stopping, and then on into Queensland; crossing invisible borders and invading new territory. Vic recalled the heat, the way his bare legs would stick to the vinyl seats in the back of the borrowed sedan, and the vibrations of the road. They spent just under two weeks in a caravan park near a tidal river. Nobody knew who John was, and nobody stopped to talk to him and ask him how he had "pulled up" after the game. Glenda spent most of the time sitting on a banana lounge, that was only partly protected from the intense sun by the caravan's open annexe; she loved reading old copies of Woman's Day that had been left in the caravan. Vic had taken up with a motley group of kids his own age, although he was forever coming back to the caravan, making sure his mother and John were still there. Often, he found his mother sleeping away the afternoon, her pale skin turning red in the heat. John stayed inside the caravan, sitting at the undersized kitchen table as if waiting for someone to join him in conversation.

There were a few outings, tourist things. Vic remembered the big pineapple, the big banana and an adventure park that was accessed via a chairlift. Each seat carried two people; Vic rode with his mother, and John rode alone. On the long drive home to Henrithvale, his mother said she wouldn't mind making a permanent move to a place with a little more sunshine, but John hated the idea, said he didn't know why everyone made "such a big deal out of fuckin' Queensland." He said their beer was like stale piss left in the sun. Vic giggled, but the glare John gave him in the rear-view mirror made him stop.

It was the only vacation they ever took. His mother had taken dozens of photos on the way up of John driving and of Vic asleep. There was even one of John and Vic standing stiffly in front of a sign welcoming travellers to Queensland, but no photos were taken on the way back. John drove hunched over the wheel most of the way home, uncoiling the closer they came to Henrithvale. By the time they were just a few hours from home, his right arm was hanging out the open window and his left hand rested on top of the steering wheel.

John had barely raised his voice the whole time they were away. Glenda said it was because he wasn't as stressed and didn't always need to do something around the farm, at the football club or for the Growers' Association. At home she had asked John if they could take more vacations, just a week every year or so to a caravan park or campsite, but John had berated her for wanting to throw money away on things they couldn't afford. Eventually she stopped asking.

The T-shirt that was wrapped around the wrench was a memento of some gorge they had visited. It had gold cursive writing across the front that read: Queensland—The Sunshine State. Vic only wore it once after they returned to Henrithvale, then stuck the T-shirt under the bottom drawer of the bedroom tallboy. He forgot about it until it was too small to be of any use. Somehow it had ended up in the machinery shed and now it kept the plumber's wrench safe.

— ★ —

Vic saw Jane returning from shopping. She stopped her car next to the shed and wound down the window, just enough for her voice to be heard.

"Thought you were going to take it easy?" There was no keeping the rain out and she brushed it from her eyes.

"That's what I'm doin'."

"It's freezing out here." She challenged.

"I'm alright. Don't notice it after a while." The shed reeked of mice and fertilizer which intensified in the foul weather. Vic didn't mind it.

"You want a coffee?"

"Nah." He squinted at her, heard the compromise in her voice and thought about the soreness in the tips of his fingers and his nose. "Actually, yeah, alright. Just give us a minute."

She wound up the window and drove the car the fifteen metres to the carport. Vic considered all the things he had dragged out of the ute; pieces of some unsolvable puzzle. He ducked his head, in a strange effort to keep dry and dashed across to the house.

In the kitchen he sat down at the table and waited for the kettle to boil while Jane packed away the shopping.

"I was talking to mum," Jane began. She briefly stopped unpacking and turned to him. He felt as if he had been lured into something. The kettle boiled and Jane poured water into each cup so that the coffee aroma washed through the room. Then she sat opposite him. Vic could see shallow lines at the corners of her eyes and the side of her mouth; he hadn't noticed them before and they seemed out of place. He had noticed similar changes in his own appearance, but they did not bother him. The changes did not seem real. Jane put her forearms on the table as if to steady her resolve and protect the space that separated them.

"Go on." It was the waiting he hated.

"You saw the brochures I got the other week?"

"Yep."

"I think," she paused. "I want to enrol in something for next year." Maybe, he thought, they could work out a deal.

"What are you thinking about?" There was more to come and he wanted to be careful.

"Nursing." Her eyes were pushed wide and she held her breath in expectation.

"If that's what you want, fair enough." He waited, then tentatively moved forward. "How would it work?"

"Not sure. I'm going to speak to an advisor tomorrow on the phone." He told her it was a good place to start and he could see she was also glad they had managed a gracious conversation. The phone rang.

"That'll be mum," Jane said and Vic stood up, feeling suddenly as if someone was watching him. He saw the lean desperado outside the foggy window, close enough to have heard everything.

Vic pushed out through the back door without thinking what he would do or say. He moved quickly around the house, but the desperado was gone. The rain worked through his shirt as he scanned the ground to his father's tree. A sudden gale turned the corner of the house behind him with a long, low cry. It prodded him forward and then vanished.

"You ain't the subtle type that's for sure." The desperado was behind him, rifle in hand. He motioned to the far-off tree with a tilt of his head and exhaled slowly. "We best take a walk."

Vic agreed and tracked after the desperado through the dense grass. They were behind the orchard of new trees. The desperado had flouted custom, was pushing into new territory and Vic did not know what he was capable of, what he might do.

Vic had no desire, no interest, in being near his father's tree, but the desperado cut a direct path over the marshy ground and Vic slogged along behind. The land here would sometimes hold water for weeks, breeding plagues of whining mosquitoes. Vic's socks and pants were soon as saturated as his shirt from the dense grass. At the tree the desperado took off his hat and emptied the brim of the water that had gathered there.

"That old boy skinned out," the desperado complained. "Thought he might. Never did like spendin' so long waitin' on somethin'."

"You're alone then," Vic asked as he glimpsed the tree. He didn't want to touch its branches or the fallen and brittle leaves that were around it. He felt a sudden trepidation and there were fumes from burning oil.

"Alone? Ain't we all." The desperado derided as he sat against the tree. He scanned the almight sky; the rain crawling through the foliage of the tree and onto his face. "This is one shit of a place. Can understand why you're so damn certain to be rid of it."

Vic kneeled in the grass as if unable to bear his own weight. He felt like a drowned man who had been brought back to life. Raindrops were running down the back of his ears, over his eyebrows and into the corners of his eyes.

"This the tree, ain't it?" Vic didn't answer. "Let me tell you somethin'." The desperado kicked at the ground with the heels of his boots. "Some years back I found myself workin' as a deputy. Had a man in a cell waitin' ta hang. Built the gallows right outside his window. Day before it was set he says he needs one more day, jus' one more to get himself right. Sheriff gives it to him. I expect that man had somethin' he was plannin' on, but at the end of his one more day there ain't nothin'. He begs and cries for jus' one more day. An' Sheriff gives it to him. This goes on near a week an' people want to see a hangin' so Sheriff tells that man his time is up. I ask this man what he is waitin' on, what he thought might happen. Know what he said?"

Vic didn't speak; but the wind felt like a hand on the side of his head.

"He says he was jus' hopin' somethin' would happen. Thought if he stayed long enough it was sure to work out. I bet he was thinkin' that even when they put that rope around his neck. Probably thinkin' it while he pissed in his pants."

"What else could he do?" Vic asked, a torrent running down inside the back of his shirt.

The desperado leaned forward.

"Coulda done anythin' he damn well wanted. Weren't nothin' more he could lose." He stood up. "Need to be goin'." He glided away from the tree in the direction of the station house that waited beyond the hills.

Vic had been close to his father's tree only one other time since the accident. It was before he and Jane were married. He wanted to show her a version of the past. He crept over to the tree as thunder broke suddenly overhead. Carefully, he leant against the tree, sitting just as the desperado had done. The rough trunk of the tree felt harsh and uncomfortable against his back. Its canopy provided little shelter. Through the downpour he could see the farmhouse and it seemed much further away than it had ever been before.

– ★ –

Vic went in the back door as Jane hung up the phone. His clothes were soaked, and he felt caught within them. He put out his arms and pulled her against him. He wasn't even sure what he was asking for or what he was offering. She pushed out of his embrace and looked down at her own clothes, now wet with the impression of him.

"What were you doing?" She was perplexed.

"Just saw a fox."

"A fox?" She didn't believe him.

"Maybe." He changed direction. "How many days a week did you say this nursing thing was?" She was still suspicious.

"I could do it part-time, Thursday and Friday, on campus," she said. It was a good compromise. He could work with it.

"Go down on Wednesday night and come back Friday night," he added. "For how long?"

"Five years, maybe six."

It could work. He could get the girls to school two days a week, take care of the lunches, cook the dinner. Maybe it would be good for him. She seemed to let him think about it, and then she took a breath and spoke quickly.

"Full-time I'd be done in three years."

"Full-time? Five days a week."

"We could stay with Mum and Dad."

"We?" What did that mean?

"The girls could go to school in Bendigo. Bigger schools, better opportunities." He wondered now if all that she was really trying to do was to find a way to leave him.

"Right." He thought they had been working to close the space. "Talk about university, but you just want to go."

"How can you always be so pigheaded?" she demanded. "This farm doesn't work anymore!"

"Doesn't work? I'm doing plenty of work."

"Don't do that, Vic. The house is old and it needs work, we're losing money every year. When will that stop? Where will the girls go to school? Where?" There was nothing for him to say and she wouldn't stay on her side of the field. "I'm not your mother. I can't just stay here—" It was a below the belt punch he didn't see coming. The suddenness of it rocked him backwards. It was as if some billowing rush had pushed him down under the water, so that he wasn't sure how to find the surface.

His mother, he knew, had stayed for him. Everything had been for him, and Jane knew it. His mother had made sure that she had suffered more so than him. And she got nothing for it, nothing. There was only Vic to know, Vic to remember, and if he wasn't here, if he didn't make something of it, then it didn't mean anything.

"My mother—" The words were barely a sound and he didn't know if he was standing or sitting, but something was climbing its way up through his chest. He clenched his hands across his heart and pulled air into his lungs with a single, laboured breath.

He could see Jane's lips were moving, forming the sound of his name, but he couldn't hear her. He charged out the door, into the rain and the hard wind. He started to walk, reeled, and then pitched towards the ute that was parked in the shed; climbed inside and drove, as if pursued, towards the orchard. The ute skidded as he rounded a turn. He overcorrected and went into a slide but held tight to the steering wheel as the ute stalled and then stopped; he heard his own loud and erratic breathing. Jane was right. She wasn't his mother.

Brian had called in the afternoon to let Vic know there was an extraordinary meeting for members of the Growers' Association. What a fucking joke it had become. Vic had immediately agreed to attend. He arrived early, as a gale blew, and sat in the ute as the light around the school building transformed into shapeless night. Brian was late. Other cars arrived but their drivers, like Vic, seemed to take Brian's absence as a sign to remain in their vehicles. When Dave Foster arrived, he parked next to Vic and then got out of his car. Emboldened, Vic got out of the ute and opened his palms to the night sky.

"Brian's not here," Vic said.

"Bullshit!" Vic could not see Dave's features, but his surprise was evident. The wind grabbed at them.

Dave pranced over to the school building and jerked at the door handle. It was locked.

"The Old Clock's gone —" He was interrupted by the brusque sound of Brian Hennan's early model FJ Holden charging into the car park.

Brian took hold of the doorframe and dragged himself out of his car; a pack started to form around him.

"Brian," Vic said loudly. "Thought you'd forgotten us."

"Well, many hands make light work, but it is my hands on which we all rely and there is simply more than I can do." Brian tucked in his shirt and closed the car door.

"Give you a hand, Brian?" Vic asked.

"Certainly. There are two boxes on the backseat that don't have legs."

Brian limped towards the school building. Vic opened the back door of Brian's car, took out a box and handed it to Dave. He had to climb onto the backseat to reach the other box.

As a boy, he had been in the backseat of Brian's car hundreds of times, going to and from local footy games and other Henrithvale events. The interior of the car had the same blandness that it had then. He remembered the times he and Dave had been in the backseat together, with Brian driving them home after a junior training. Dave would often try to pluck a hair from Brian's head.

"I will thank you, Master Foster, to keep your hands to yourself," was Brian's restrained response. It would send them into fits of muffled hilarity.

Inside the school, Brian was busy making sure the lights were on and the heater was working. The room was filling with the farmers and local business owners who Brian had telephoned. Vic presumed that Brian's mood was the result of someone who had tired of his calls and told him in some obscene way to refrain from telephoning. Vic and Dave started rearranging the chairs, and then Vic heard the sound of Brian's car. He had driven away.

"Reckon he mighta got himself a woman," Dave ventured unfavourably.

People broke into groups and began to hypothesise as to where Brian might be. Vic sat and thought how easy it would be if Brian never returned. Without him the Growers' Association would not hold, and the football club, already condemned, would not receive a stay. Twenty minutes later Brian drove back into the school car park and laboured into the classroom. People sat down, and Brian made his way to his seat, pressed record on the tape recorder and gave the date. He paused and sat upright in his chair.

"Don't reckon we'll get any more," Vic said from his seat.

"Well, it is disappointing given the gravity of our situation, but we will soldier on." Brian took attendance and began organising his paper work, moving sheets from one pile to the next and then putting them back in the same pile. There was discernible unease, something Brian seemed to think gave him an advantage.

"Those of you familiar with the Henrithvale region might be surprised to know the area was once home to Aboriginal people." He cleared his throat. "My understanding is that they belonged to a particular group known as Wergaia." Vic saw a lot of perplexed faces. "Be that as it may, this once happy hunting ground was no longer thought to contain a trace of them. However, in recent months—"

"Is there a point to this, Brian?" Rob Masterson had come to argue.

"Yes, Robert there is a point to it." Brian slashed back at him and sat up in his chair and adjusted his glasses. "The point is this: a sizeable part of Henrithvale is being assessed by people from a respected university to see if it qualifies as a place of cultural value belonging to those Aboriginal people." Brian was impressed with himself.

"Do they want it back?" Rob mocked. Someone snorted.

"No doubt some far-flung descendant just might. That, however, is neither here nor there," Brian said, without humour. "Think. A positive finding for such an assessment would lead to Henrithvale being marked as a place of cultural importance and value for these people."

"And?"

"Robert, you are bewildering at times." Brian, Vic thought, was not out of place at the front of a classroom. "In such circumstances it would be near impossible to construct a dam of any sort lest something more is lost. Without the prospect of a dam there is no good reason for the requisition of irrigation leases."

Rob brushed his hands over his face as his restless feet tapped a quick beat on the floor. Then he snapped at Brian.

"You called everyone out to say, once upon a time, some Abos lived here, and you reckon everythin'll be alright?" Vic could feel the room tighten and strain. If this was all Brian had to say, it was a terrible miscalculation to call a meeting. "Are you even gunna say what university it is?" Nobody said anything.

Vic remembered the stories about how it was Rob's great-great grandfather who had been among those who made sure there were no longer any First Nations People in the area. When Vic and Rob and Dave were in the fourth grade a harsh drought had dried up many of the small dams in the area for the first time in more than a century. The dam on the Masterson's property had revealed the bones of fifteen First Nations People. Rob had taken two of the skulls into school for show-and-tell. Mrs Summerset, a tender but strongminded woman, who was at the school only a year had confiscated them and called the police. The bones were taken away to be scrutinized and catalogued and the story disappeared. There had been a small article about it in the regional paper, saying it was not known how the bones got into the Masterson's dam. And there was a photo of a youthful Rob, taken at home before Mrs Summerset's intervention, holding some of the bones in his hands.

A school excursion was organised after Rob's antics. They went out to the quarry to see what remained of the rock art. Mrs Summerset talked about the people who had stencilled their hands on the outcrops. She said they had lived here for thousands and thousands of years, and that they lived in harmony with the land and with the river. A few months later, without fanfare, she left the area.

"What exactly does it mean, Brian?" It was Doc's voice that, as usual, was trying to avoid confrontation. He must have come in late and was standing at the back of the room, his thin face unshaved.

"I first contacted the university some months ago." Brian announced. "But I only received word yesterday that something might come of it. You should all know this and know it clearly." Brian's back straightened, and his hands slapped down on the table in front of him; papers floated to the floor. "We don't have the strength to land a knockout blow. If we are going to overcome this it will be by scraping forward one inch at a time." He challenged Rob, pointing directly at him. "Here is another inch or two."

Rob stood up with a sudden jerk and pointed at Brian.

"You're a fuckin' idiot, Hennan! Abos and a fuckin' dam?" He stormed towards the door and stopped. "It's irrigation leases they're takin', that's the reality," he added, turning around to scowl at Brian again. "The dam is all in that fuckin' empty head of yours." He pulled open the door and left, letting it slam closed behind him. Nobody moved. Vic could hear the wind outside.

"United we stand, divi—" Brian began.

"There was another article on the front page of the paper today," Doc interjected from the back. Vic watched as he weaved his way across the room with his long legs to hand Brian the paper. Brian held it up for everyone to see the headline: "A Dam Mess."

There had been too many such articles for Vic to remember. From the day the government began the compulsory requisition of irrigation leases, there had been rumours it was part of a bigger plan to dam the valley and that would put Henrithvale underwater. Vic didn't believe that there was necessarily much to it, but the papers loved it.

"Is that it then, Brian?" Dave spoke for everybody.

"There is something else you need to be made aware of, something that has come to light today." Brian looked at his paperwork. "This, I should qualify, did not reach me through official channels. Nevertheless, our government, in its infinite wisdom," he took in a steadying breath, "has apparently given the green light to apple and pear imports from China." The room was still. There wasn't the energy to rise up anymore. Vic felt it in himself. He surveyed the room, looking at all the men, most with eyes red from lack of sleep, none of them making any real money. The details of the deal didn't matter, the quality of the product didn't matter. Cheaper imports were dangerous. They would erode the market share of local produce. There might still be room for local growers; there just wouldn't be as much room as there had been.

In the years when Henrithvale was a successful club the notion of losing, always losing, was not something they ever needed to consider. If they didn't get a premiership one year, then it would definitely be next year or the year after. When Vic started playing senior football the club's fortunes had declined, but the expectations were not surrendered so easily. As the distance between premiership victories lengthened, there was a changing of coaches, a changing of approaches, an urgency to find out what it was that had stopped the club from winning. There wasn't the money there once was, from sponsors or from success. Vic sensed behind it all was a fear that something was rotten, something that could not be fixed. Soon came the corrosive losses, by eighty points, one hundred and twenty points, a hundred and fifty points; week after week and year after year.

All of those great things that Vic had watched John do, watched Henrithvale achieve, for so many years, now seemed to belong only to the past. Nothing was said, but there was an awakening, an awareness that Henrithvale would not win, could not win. Every week and every season had offered the chance to start again, but the feeling that winning was impossible became an infection that festered, sickening any chance of success. Vic felt it in his own game. He started to notice how big the field was, how far away the goals were, how sluggishly he moved. The kind of victory that might announce a return to those golden years never happened. His pre-game confidence was continually taunted into submission, only to re-emerge in the days after to carry him into the next game; but there were too many games that Henrithvale didn't win, too many times they were unable to hold on. Every week Brian spoke with passion, pleading with his players to give more, but they could not and did not know how.

"I'm going to say something now," Brian focussed on the children's pictures that decorated the walls. "My family, like many of you here now, have been in the Henrithvale area for generations. There were droughts, fire and everything else to contend with, but they pushed on. They made something out of nothing. Every time they got knocked down, they got back up. We can do the same. Communities like Henrithvale made this country what it is, made us who we are—"

"Brian," Dave interrupted. "Let's just call it a night." Dave's voice was stressed. "Yeah?" Brian had little time to agree, people started to leave.

Vic and Dave helped Brian stack away the chairs, then carried Brian's boxes back to his car. They watched him drive away in silence. The car park was empty except for them. Dave got into his car, started the engine and wound down his window.

"Dunno why he said that, ya know, about imports." Dave was irritated, his face illuminated by the interior light in his car. "It was like a kick in the ball sack. All he'll fuckin' do is make people sign on the dotted line." Vic tapped the top of Dave's car.

"I dunno." Vic said. "I dunno." He watched Dave drive away before he climbed into the cab of the ute. He started the engine, switched on the headlights.

– ★ –

The desperado standing a few metres away, squinting in the glare. It had been startling to see him away from the station house, but away from the farm altogether gave him an autonomy that scared Vic.

Vic left the engine running and got out of the ute.

"Horse'd never do that to a man," the desperado said and stepped away from the lights towards Vic. "You quit so damn quick it's surprisin' you learned to walk."

There was a change in the desperado. He stood closer to Vic so that Vic could take in the smokiness of burning autumn leaves that emanated from him. In the evening beyond them Vic knew there was something strange, something destructive. He looked back towards the ute.

"I'd be leavin' too if I was you," the desperado said turning his head towards the gloom.

Vic locked the door and drove away. He knew at home Sarah and Emily would be waiting and glad to see him. When the road curved, he saw his father's tree in the headlights, haunting the paddock. Vic thought for the first time about how easy it would be on such a night as this for a car to slide off the road and into a tree; maybe that would be alright, maybe it would be the best thing he could do.

Vic sat at the kitchen table, his hands wrapped tightly around a freshly poured coffee. The morning had arrived with guttural thunder. He watched through the kitchen window as battered clouds marched through the valley like remnants of a retreating army. It was early and there was barely light in the day. Jane and the girls were still in bed. This is what John had done most mornings. Whenever Vic inhaled brewing coffee it came with a picture of John sitting just where he was now. He had to check the dams. The gauge near the orchard gave him the feeling they would be near full and he could not remember the last time he had to pump water out of a dam.

The phone rang as the handle on the coffee cup broke off and the cup hit the corner of the table and smashed on the floor. He put the handle on the table, got up, wiped his mouth and hurried over to answer the phone.

"Hello." Vic watched the coffee vapours from the broadening pool on the kitchen floor.

"Vic, Brian Hennan calling." He waited as if he expected to be interrupted. "Now this is going to sound like you are getting the run around—"

"Brian... Brian, just save everyone the drive." The coffee had spread and seeped into the gaps in the floorboards

"This is of the utmost significance."

"Another bloody meeting. Christ, Brian." There is no such thing as dying with dignity.

"Yes, Vic, another meeting." Brian saw dissent as weakness.

Vic thought about the desperado in the car park; about the need for borders and the danger of changing the rules. He wondered if he should keep away from Jane, from the girls, lest the desperado work into that space.

"Alright," he said, capitulating, and hung up the phone. Jane was behind him.

"Something wrong?" she asked.

"Dropped the bloody coffee cup." Vic made his way over to the kitchen sink and found a sponge and a tea towel.

"Who was on the phone?" Jane was huddled inside a pink dressing gown.

"Brian. Wants to have another meetin' tonight." Vic knelt on the floor and set about cleaning up the coffee and broken cup.

"Another meeting? What happened last night?" Her questions said that she didn't believe him. Where did she think he was going?

"Brian still reckons it's all about how the government wants to build a dam. He reckons he can block it because Henrithvale has Aboriginal significance."

Jane rolled her eyes. He got up and put the broken pieces of the coffee cup in the bin.

"Plans for the day?" he asked, wiping his hands on his jeans.

"I've got that appointment to speak to a student adviser at the university. They'll call at eleven." Her voice pushed forward a feeble confidence.

"Right."

"How's your head?" Jane asked.

"It's alright. Not too much damage I reckon."

She reached out a hand. He took it in his, but wasn't sure what she wanted him to know. Perhaps, he thought, she was telling him that he had played well, he had done his best, but he had lost, and that was okay.

"I was looking for my high school results last night. I found some old photos. You and your mum." Her words were careful. He felt a sharp pain in his chest. "You look about eight or nine."

She went into the lounge room and returned with a shoebox. Vic and Jane sat at the table together. Vic had no memory of the photos being taken and no memory of having seen the photos before; he didn't know how they had escaped John's purge. In the photos he was happy and so was his mother; but not just for the sake of the picture. Yet, it was an unremembered day. Who had taken the photos? John? Not likely.

"That's great." He couldn't believe it and kept a tight hold on the photos in case they were just the workings of his imagination. Jane squeezed his hand again. Perhaps there were other photos yet to be found, something more to uncover.

– ★ –

The day remained unmoved, buried under winter clouds. Vic spent most of it in the orchard, his thoughts on the photos Jane had found and the life she was planning without him. The weather made his skin ache and he felt as if he were collapsing. He trudged back to the house in the early afternoon. Jane was standing in the doorway between the lounge room and the kitchen, a coffee cup in her hands, her eyes puffy. There was a collection of brochures on the bench next to an envelope marked La Trobe University.

"Day alright?" he asked. There were freshly washed dishes in the drying rack. He took up a tea towel and began drying plates. No answer.

"How'd you go with the university?" Jane hunched and turned her back on him. Vic recognised the signals. When they'd first met, she used to do it more often: feel beaten by something, cry, turn her back, and wait for his reassurance. It disappeared more-or-less once the girls were born.

"Jane?"

He dropped the tea towel and put his hand on her thin shoulders, then she embraced him. She let him rub her back and kiss her on the head. Then she wiped her eyes with her forearm, trying not to spill her coffee.

"It was a stupid idea. I couldn't do full-time, even if I got in. Not with the girls. Part-time maybe." She leaned her head against his chest, and the freshly brewed coffee mixed in with her washed-out perfume from yesterday. "They said I had a better shot at TAFE, but I should do a short course before that. Refresh skills. I know how to write." He had a feeling of confidence akin to that which comes in a footy game when an opponent was out of run and the game was still to be won. He didn't want her to see it.

"I need to get the girls," she said, pulling away from him, but in a way that Vic thought showed appreciation for his efforts. Jane swallowed the last of her coffee and put the empty cup on the bench. Then, with her thumbs, she cleared away the tears from under her eyes. When she was gone, Vic got in the shower with a feeling that he might be able to make things work for another year.

The girls were crying before they opened the back door. They were hurt and confused. It reminded Vic of a younger version of himself.

"Daddy!" Sarah ran in and clung to his waist, pressing her face against his stomach. Emily was close behind. He rubbed their heads and comforted them. Jane came inside, holding onto a letter in one hand and her car keys in the other, a handbag slung over her shoulder.

"What's goin' on?" Vic asked. Emily tilted her head back and sobbed.

"They're closing the school," she said.

"What?"

"Sent this letter home to all the parents," Jane said waving the letter at him. "It's from the Department of Education." She dropped her keys and handbag on the table and started reading it aloud. "'We regret to advise that Henrithvale Consolidated School will be permanently closed at the conclusion of the current school year. A decline in enrolments over several years, combined with poor future intake projections makes the school no longer economically viable.'"

"This is bullshit," Vic uttered. He knew what it meant.

"Listen to this part." She found the section she was looking for with her finger. "'We regret any inconvenience this may cause you and your family.'"

"Any inconvenience!" He wanted to lash out, punch at the wall, but the girls were still wrapped around his waist.

"They've got it all figured out." She continued reading: "'The Department of Education has agreed to provide a shuttle service to the nearest school provided ten or more students require the service.'"

"What does that mean? They want the kids to spend hours a day on the fuckin' bus?"

"Vic, language."

Jane had never been a fan of profanity. Vic wondered if she would have been better off with Brian Hennan. Then he found himself wondering why Jane wasn't looking to push her advantage. She had him now; it was finished.

He knelt down so that he was at eye level with Emily and Sarah.

"I don't wanna go to a new school," Emily sniffed. Her nose and mouth reminded him of his mother. "It's not fair."

"There is a meeting tomorrow morning at the school," Jane said.

"It's meeting after meeting these days," Vic muttered, bawling his hands into fists and raising them to the sides of his head. Emily let him go, wiping her own tears, and Vic stood up. "Someone crosses the bloody street and there needs to be a meeting."

"Daddy," Emily said. "I don't wanna go on a bus for three hours every day."

"We'll work somethin' out. Alright." Fuck Brian. He should've known. No. No, not just Brian.

Vic knew that for Jane the school carried more weight than the irrigation leases, but Brian would never see it that way, wouldn't understand. He was a traditionalist. For him, a man was the head of his family and his Word was law; his wife and children deferred to him out of a desire to please or appease. Jane wasn't like that, not anymore. But Vic didn't want it that way either, not all the time. The loss of the school would give her a momentum he would not be able to stop. It didn't matter anymore who was to blame, it was all the same, fucked.

He left early for the Growers' Association meeting. He had no answer if the school closed and Jane, he thought, knew it. There was no need to say anything. Perhaps she was giving him opportunity to abdicate. Still, he did not know what a future outside of Henrithvale would offer. She had, he thought, given him good reason to believe that her vision of Bendigo did not include him. The loss of the farm, the town, and the marriage could only lead to an end. Perhaps that was what was needed. Perhaps it was he that carried John's transgressions, and he must suffer for them.

The foreboding of late afternoon hung over the town, emanating from the outlying hills. There were pockets of mist spreading across the road. He wondered if Brian had a solution, not likely. He knew he couldn't panic and say something he couldn't take back, he had to wait and see.

The ute cruised past the school and Vic saw that only Brian's car was there and so he pressed on into town to see Herbert and Edna.

The door to the shop was locked, but the interior light was on and Vic could see Herbert inside, stirring the dust about with his feet. Vic tapped on the door. Herbert saw him and trailed over.

"Here he is," Herbert opened the door enough for Vic to come in. There were a few boxes on the floor.

"Redecorating, Jack?" Vic teased.

Herbert managed to force a single syllable laugh in return, but his face was greyish. He continued to poke at the empty shelves.

"Violet has come up," he finally said, kicking the empty boxes into a corner. "She's with Edna out back."

"Everything alright, Jack?" A stupid question.

Herbert seemed about to speak and then stopped. He faced Vic.

"Look, I didn't want to say anything. Thought I'd just send a letter." He started tapping his left foot in a quick rhythm then stopped, his voice contrite.

"We'll go down to the city with Violet tomorrow."

"Yeah, you said you were heading down for a while."

Herbert's eyes told Vic things had changed.

"We're moving down until Edna…" Herbert held his breath and then swallowed it. "Move Edna into a hospice and I'll stay with Violet. Keep it that way."

"Hello, Dad?" Vic turned around to see Violet, Herbert's and Edna's second-oldest daughter. She was taller than Vic remembered, her hair a shiny red. She recognised him but wasn't sure why. "Oh, my goodness! Vic? How are you?" She embraced him and he kissed her on the cheek.

"Yeah, can't complain. All's good."

"It's nice to see you." She was overly sincere, but she made the best pumpkin soup he'd ever had; butternut pumpkin and nutmeg. He remembered her making it when he would visit but Violet would never part with the recipe. "So you have two daughters now?"

"Yep, Emily and Sarah. They're nine and seven."

"Wonderful, just wonderful." Vic knew Violet had never married. She wasn't interested. She turned her attention to Herbert. "The soup is done, Dad."

"Alright, Love," Herbert reassured her.

"It was great to see you again, Vic." Violet reached out her left hand and squeezed his right arm. Vic felt like he was still a shy boy she was taking care of.

"Yeah, you too." Violet disappeared back through the doorway and into the house.

"Haven't said anything to anyone," Herbert stared at the floor. "Think I prefer it that way."

"Yeah, yeah alright." He was the same; a victory is always shared but defeat is a solitary event.

More changes, Vic thought, another loss of permanence. The fragility scared him, but he couldn't be angry, not at Herbert and Edna. He didn't think he would still be alive now if they hadn't been around after his mother died.

"Come by in the morning, Vic. We'll leave around eleven." Herbert opened the door for him, and Vic left.

He drove the empty road. There had barely been any light in the day and nightfall scavenged what it could find. The first time he had driven Jane around Henrithvale, a week after meeting her at Doc's wedding, he showed her the footy ground, the pub, and the school. It bucketed down the whole time. They had a picnic near the orchard under a tarp he stretched between two trees. He remembered feeling like his mother was proud of him, like he had a lifetime to make things right.

Vic wondered if anyone else had agreed to come in to another Growers' Association meeting, but when he pulled into the car park, at least a dozen cars were there. Did they already know about the school closure? He parked next to Dave's car and went into the classroom. The chairs were already set out but there was none of the other paraphernalia, no pamphlets or forms or newsletters. Vic exchanged a few greetings as he crossed the room to where Dave, June and others were talking about the school closure. People around the room stood in solemn groups talking in voices of disbelief, stating their objections and recalling their own school days. He noticed pencil shavings on the floor and the hands of the wall clock frozen at five-fifteen. More and more Vic just wanted it to be done with.

"Bit late, Vic." Dave winked. "I got me fuckin' sleepin' bag in the car. Save me comin' back tomorra." He sipped quickly at a cup of tea, dirt from his hands marking the battered cup.

"Here's Brian." Dave said signalling towards the door with eyebrows raised as Brian limped towards them with the same stern determination he had when he was about to give the three-quarter-time address. He was wearing brown pants and a pastel cream shirt with a brown floral tie. Dave let out part of a wolf-whistle that Brian stopped with a glare.

"We'll get things underway if we can, please." Brian sat at the front of the room. He seemed to want a stage or raised platform. "It is right on six, but those who come late can learn a valuable lesson in organisation." People sat down or stood, leaning against the wall near the door. Brian held some papers in his hands, was about to speak and then noticed that the record button on his tape player had not been pressed. He came around the desk, leaned over the tape player in an action that Vic found excruciating, and set the tape in motion. Then he resumed his seat. "Before we call the meeting to order I would like to thank you for attending on such short notice."

Rob Masterson, soaked in the stench of beer, was waiting near the door. His thumbs hooked onto the pockets of his jeans. Vic was surprised to see him. Rob, Vic thought, was just another version of John, one that couldn't kick a ball and thus didn't have the same prestige.

"Yesterday I announced that I had word the federal government was opening up markets to China for the import of apples and pears." Brian enjoyed the pageantry. "Today announcements were made that show this will indeed be the case. Grim news." He searched the room, but there was little in the way of a response. "However," he checked the papers in his hands, "there will be a further announcement tomorrow that this opening of markets will be met with increased subsidies for Australian growers." He pressed the broad brown tie against his chest. "To put that in layman's terms, your income, your market share, will be guaranteed. Indexed."

"Bullshit!" Rob called out. Brian ignored him.

"I can tell you that the Farmer's Unions at a state and federal level, together with the Growers' Association, have put in long and hard hours on this." Vic watched as people leaned back in their chairs, looking at each other for confirmation.

Still, Vic did not see it as enough to diminish the school closure. He carefully examined his hands. The palms were still dirty and so were his fingernails. His mother used to scrub them every night before he went to bed until he was twelve. He protested and resisted her doing so but was glad for it.

"There is another matter I need to address." Brian raised his voice until he again had the attention of the room. "No doubt you have heard, in one way or another, that the decision has been made to close the school." He scoffed, and his jowls made him sound horse-like.

Somebody behind Vic booed and it made Vic wonder if they understood how significant such a move would be. There had been articles in the paper all year about falling enrolments and the urgent need for repairs to school buildings, and not just in Henrithvale.

"There will be a meeting here for all concerned tomorrow morning at nine sharp." Brian leaned forward, wagging his pointer finger, his voice exuding confidence. "These so-and-sos in government need to understand that Henrithvale will not be intimidated." Vic looked sideways at Dave's grim face. Maybe Rob Masterson was right.

Vic left as soon as the meeting had finished. He rubbed his hands together and started the ute. The heater in the ute never seemed to do more than circulate the cold; it was like sitting in a breezy icebox. He drove hunched forward as the windscreen fogged over; he could see the house lights as he approached the driveway. The farm, Jane, the football club and now the school were a knot that he couldn't unravel.

He parked in the carport. As he climbed out of the ute, he thought he heard something, someone, behind him, but he couldn't see anything in the night.

Jane had set aside a plate for him, and he ate it while watching TV with the girls. There was no comforting their confusion. Later, he read to them while they were in bed, a few chapters from Watership Down. He had started it months ago and didn't know if it would take but they adored it. He wasn't sure they understood everything that was going on, Sarah asked a lot of questions, but they understood enough that he had to leave the rabbits that roamed the farm to do as they please. His mother read it to him when he was ten and it became a shared adventure. When he turned out the light in their room, they didn't seem any more reassured. He didn't want to tell them it was a feeling they should get used to, not yet.

He went into the lounge room and Jane was sitting on the couch in front of the TV. He sat down next to her. He had an odd sense that his mother was in another room, and that when he had to leave the house in which he had spent his entire life, he would leave her there behind.

"I'll give Mum a call tomorrow," Jane said. "Get her to find something out about schools in her area."

"Got that meeting tomorrow, yeah?"

"It's not up in the air, Vic. it won't change because you or Brian Hennan makes a speech." He winced and couldn't bring himself to face her. "What will it take, Vic? What?" She was fierce.

He stood up, wanting to say something that would make her see she was wrong, that she owed him, that he was the one being cheated and that she was in cahoots with the banks and the politicians. But there was only a harrowing sadness, a betrayal, and humiliation. He put the plate in the kitchen sink and went to bed.

A melancholy had infested the house and it fostered a lethargy that Vic could not ward off. He watched the rain make the world beyond the window as indistinct as it felt. He still hadn't checked the dams, but it didn't seem like Jane would be influenced by him declaring there was ample water available for the coming season. He knew a sudden abundance of water wouldn't pay off debt that had long passed the point of no return. Yet, he could not relinquish the idea he must go on. Jane drove the girls to school after they said whimpering goodbyes.

His grandfather had always said, "you make your own luck." For a long time, he had believed it, but not anymore. He wondered why it was that fortune gave to some and not others. If the requisition of the irrigation leases had happened to John, it would have been a blessing—for him and his mother at least. Then, perhaps, his mother might not have died. It was the cancer that killed her, but John was the cause.

The phone rang four times before he got up to answer it because he knew who it would be.

"Good morning, this is Brian Hennan." There was something of trepidation in Brian's voice.

"Yes, Brian."

"As you're no doubt aware there has been circulation of a letter announcing the closure of the school."

"Yeah, I read it last night." He pressed the receiver against his ear and noticed the blotchy oil marks on the ceiling above the stove were larger than he recalled.

"There is a meeting this morning at the school. We need to show those powers-that-be this school—"

"I'll be there." Vic could hear Brian thinking, crafting some more words he clearly wanted Vic to have.

"There is a feeling, I can tell you this much, that the end of the school might push people to make hasty decisions."

"I'll see you at the meeting, Brian." Vic kept the receiver pressed against his ear long after Brian ended the call, listening to the harbingers caught in static.

– ★ –

Vic bolted to the machinery shed. Once he was inside the rain turned to hail, thick and hard, cutting in sideways with the churning wind. There was nothing for him to do, he realised, nothing he wanted to do. He sat on the fertilizer bags piled along the wall. If he left this place, left this town, he wouldn't be anything, anyone.

He stayed in the machinery shed until it was time to go to the meeting and then drove to the school with the hail battering the ute. Jane was waiting for him under the eaves by the main entrance, but he arrived just as parents were being guided into an empty classroom. A plump woman in a casual black suit stood at the door and welcomed them individually with a voice that promised familiarity and understanding.

"Hi," she began, forthright and making deliberate eye contact with as many people as she could. "My name is Roxy Pemberton and I'm here from the Department of Education along with my colleague,

Anthony Hamilton." She acknowledged, with the sweep of her arm, a tall thin man in a light brown suit and poorly shaped goatee. "We are here to assist and advise parents and care providers during school transitions." She paused. "I just want to start off by saying what a beautiful town you have."

Vic thought there would be more animosity, but he soon got the feeling that people just wanted to know how it would all work, so they could adapt and move on. The room was smaller than the one used for the Growers' Association meetings and aside from himself there were few fathers present. It was too late to get out. Jane, seated next to him, had turned in her chair so that her back was partially to him and he could not see her face. Yet she had wanted him here, he knew, for this was an intervention, a public revelation and denouncement.

"I'll be here every second week for two months to answer questions and help you and the little ones make choices that will help with positive transition," Roxy finished, resting her hands on her stomach.

She waited for questions.

There was silence. Brian Hennan stood, raising his hand from the back of the room. Roxy invited him to speak. Brian introduced himself by giving the full list of his Henrithvale duties; the intonations in his voice changed, as they often did when he spoke to women, and hovered somewhere between impatient and affronted. Vic doubted he was aware of it. Roxy was unfazed.

"As someone who has lived in Henrithvale his entire life, someone who attended this very school, as did my father and his father before him, the school closure comes as quite a shock."

"It shouldn't. The process has been open and public, but I understand your feelings of confusion—"

"There is no confusion here, young lady." His chin jutted out a little. "There is a fair amount of anger, but tell me this, as this town fights for its very survival against a hostile government—"

"Sit down, Brian," an irritated voice called out and others applauded.

"Brian," Roxy interrupted. "These are not questions I can answer." Her voice had a determination about it that made Vic pay attention. She'd had this conversation before.

Brian adjusted the waist of his pants.

"My role is to assist with transitions," she continued.

"You're here, you're from the department, you answer the questions!" Brian demanded.

Anthony stood next to Roxy, raising his hands to quash Brian's disruption.

"The decision to close a school is never taken lightly," he said quickly in a nasal voice.

"Do you have any idea, fella, how long this school has been here?" Whenever Brian called someone "fella" it meant he was angry. It was his way of swearing.

"Our role is not as debaters or messengers between you and the department, our role is to assist parents and care providers." Anthony, Vic thought, had practiced these words.

Roxy and Anthony answered other questions and Brian, standing with his hand raised was ignored, his discord suffocated. This was not his place. Forms and booklets were handed out, and some parents lined up after the meeting for their chance to be given specific guidance.

Brian lined up too, irritated, and keen to harass Roxy and Anthony. Vic had an unexpected urge to stand next to him, but Jane pulled at his arm. They went outside where the hail had stopped. Jane was clutching at an information booklet. Vic sensed a determination in her stance, in the way she set her shoulders. There would be no more waiting. She would, he thought, be resolute in her demands.

"I'm going to have a coffee," she said folding the information booklet into her bag.

"Yeah, okay." There was a line of ants moving across the wall above the school's main entrance.

"We can talk later." Vic knew that she was looking directly at him but he did not want to look at her.

He headed to the ute and drove straight into town, stopping outside the general store. There was a faded, handwritten 'closed' sign taped to the front window. As he sat in the ute, Herbert appeared at the front door of the shop. Edna, supported by Violet, came after him. She looked small, shrunken. As Herbert locked up the store, Violet guided Edna into the backseat of a car.

Vic got out of the ute, leaving his door open, and approached the car.

Edna was sitting on the backseat, wrapped in blankets, with only her head and hands showing. There were bags and boxes packed around her.

"You headin' out for the day, Ed?"

Edna's eyes were watery, and he wasn't sure she could see him. She raised her head, trying to bring words up, her breath stank of decay; she just didn't have the strength anymore.

"It's alright, Ed," he reassured. "You'll be alright." He remembered her arm around his shoulders in the months after his mother's death. He remembered her washing his clothes and the money she would put in his pocket. She had said very little during this time, but he knew she was there. He wanted to thank her for her love, for her kindness, but there didn't seem to be any way he could do that.

"Dad's given me your number, and here is my card," Violet said behind him. Vic stood up and took the card from Violet, her name on one side and the brand of the United Methodist Church stamped on the other. She was too casual, too easy-going, she made the event normal.

Herbert came closer and shook hands with Vic.

"Here he is. Good lad, good lad."

Vic felt trivial, like he did when he heard John on a rant, when he heard the sounds of things break and his mother's voice scared and calling at John to stop. These things did not die. He wanted to go home, hide in the wardrobe and wait for the morning when the day would start anew.

Violet helped Herbert into the car. Vic carefully closed Edna's door. Then stood away from the car and let it go. He got into the ute and started driving back home. He was no more than a hundred metres out of town when he pulled over to the side of the road and vomited, dry retching into the grass until his stomach cramped; above him the sky was turbulent and boundless and unconquerable.

Vic returned home and had a strong coffee. He wanted to put down some fertilizer for the trees. He had called Dave the night before and organised a time to meet him at the gate with his tractor. There had been so many times after his mother's death that he stayed a night or two with Herbert and Edna. He would go into the shop after school, sometimes instead of school, and Herbert would find him something to do: take inventory, stack shelves, clear out the back shed and so on. Vic never asked to stay. It was always Edna who would say something like, "Stop in here tonight, better that way." Vic never spoke to John about it. Edna told him not to worry, that she would take care of it. They only spoke of John in passing as if describing an event or a pattern. Everything was about the farm, the weather, the football club or events and people around Henrithvale.

Vic wondered if Jane knew about Herbert and Edna and if it was just something else that told her the town was finished. He didn't want to think about it, there was nothing that could be done now. He still had the trees.

When Vic opened the back door, William Mulholland was waiting for him, resplendent in his grey suit; no button or thread was unaccounted for. His hair was neatly parted on the left side of his head, and his shoes, a polished black, seemed as if they were made of glass.

"Top of the morning to you, Vic." His voice had a merry swing and he held up his left palm, while the right kept a firm grip on his umbrella. "I come in peace, I come in peace."

Vic felt as if he were trapped. He also had a sense the desperado was near, not just watching but on the verge of acting, and Vic was not certain against whom he would act.

Mulholland crept forward.

"The way we last parted was not in the best of spirits and I've come to make amends."

"I'm busy," Vic said.

"No doubt you are. And aren't we all in some way or another."

Vic needed to walk around him to get to the machinery shed where he'd left the ute. The wind dropped leaving an unbearable stillness. Mulholland had him hemmed in.

"Just a few minutes, Vic, is all I ask, just a few minutes of your time." There was something vicious lurking around Mulholland's words.

"The ute's in the shed." Vic pointed behind Mulholland. "I need to load it and get to work. That's all the time you've got." He veered around Mulholland and moved at a quick pace.

"You're a hard man, Vic, I'll give you that." Mulholland was beside him. He used his long-handled umbrella as a walking stick. "No doubt you have to be. However, on this occasion it's not in your best interests."

Vic quickened his pace, didn't avoid the shallow brown puddles, reached the shed and put on the rigging gloves he had left on top of the work bench. The stench of mice had subsided with the clear skies. He started loading the fertilizer bags into the back of the ute. They were stacked five high against the shed wall; certified organic but still unappealing. He wriggled a bag forward, wrapped his arms around it so it balanced on his thighs and then scuttled over to the ute where he heaved the bag onto the ute's tray.

"I won't lie to you, Vic, like some would, and tell you that I am only thinking of you. I'm not. There is plenty in this for me too."

Vic dropped another bag of fertilizer into the back of the ute with a thud and then put his hands on his hips and arched his back.

"If there wasn't, you wouldn't be here," he responded as he crossed back to the fertilizer bags.

"It's not the money that I care for." Mulholland confided. "What I want you to see, Vic, is that what is best for me is also what is best for you; and most importantly best for your little girls."

Vic picked up a bag of fertilizer.

"And I should believe that?" It was the talk of slick bureaucrats.

When Vic dropped the last bag onto the tray, it sent a great puff of dusty residue into the air. Mulholland leaned on his umbrella and continued.

"You've got nothing to bargain with: no school, no football club. Don't sink with the ship, there's no dignity in it." A sudden burst of hail tapped on the roof of the shed.

Vic held his breathe, braced, then lifted the draw-bar of the two-wheeled fertilizer spreader and shuffled backwards, pulling the spreader towards the ute and hitching it to the tow bar. He took off his gloves and tossed them through the ute's open window and onto the passenger seat.

"You know how things will work out?" Vic challenged him. "What'll happen if we sell and what'll happen if we don't sell?"

"I can all but guarantee it, Vic."

"I need to get to work," Vic said.

Mulholland extended his hand. Vic could not defy custom and took it in his own.

"So be it, Vic. So be it. Go on then, take care of those precious apples. I'll be seeing you." Mulholland bid him farewell.

Vic reversed the ute out of the machinery shed and drove towards the orchard. Mulholland might have watched him go, but Vic did not look back.

He parked near the lower gate that connected his property to Dave's, just near the bottom of the orchard; leaned his shoulder against the door and shut his eyes. Dave would be there soon enough with his tractor.

Suddenly the door was jerked open and he fell out of the cab and landed on the muddy ground. He turned around and expected to hear Dave make a joke, but it was the desperado.

"I seen it an' I don't believe it." The desperado reached down and pulled Vic to his feet by the lapels of his shirt. "Jus' what you playin' at?" The desperado was agitated; his hands were enormous, and they held Vic in place.

"Get your hands off me." Vic struggled to break free from the grip but he couldn't get any leverage. His feet were barely touching the ground. He could see the underside of the desperado's hat and the inky stains that marked it. Then the desperado shoved Vic back against the ute, as to make an assessment and measure the fight Vic had in him.

"That thing you was talkin' to, all cordial, that's jus' the thing that has been troublin' you." The desperado spat on the ground and kept Vic in place with his eyes.

"Mulholland?"

"It don't matter none what his name is. I seen him a hun'red times before. You can't see that? You can't see what he is? And you holdin' his hand like a deal is done." The desperado's eyes narrowed and he turned his head slightly to the left.

"What if he's right?" Vic asked.

"The hell he is!" The desperado braced, so that his left foot was still forward but his weight was on his right leg. His hands balled into each other.

"There isn't much to choose from in case you haven't noticed." Vic said, ready to crouch down to protect himself. "Stay here alone and starve, or sell up and go with Jane."

"You go and there ain't no comin' back."

"Fuck it!" Vic turned and pounded his fists down on the bonnet of the ute. The desperado put his right hand on Vic's left shoulder.

"You're waitin' for somethin' ain't gonna come. Ain't nothin' or no one gonna save you." Vic buried his head in his hands, felt the desperado's hand fall away from his shoulder and looked up to see him turn away and walk in amongst the apple trees.

"Fuck!" Vic pounded his palms down on the bonnet of the ute.

Dave was almost alongside him before Vic heard the tractor. Vic spun around wildly. Dave turned off the engine.

"Don't reckon that'll do it. Give it a big fuckin' kick, that'll get it done."

Vic felt his face flush.

Dave leaned back in his seat and scratched at the back of his neck.

"Shit times these. Can't do a fuckin' thing that works."

Vic scanned the landscape and saw the desperado among the trees. He had raised his hands to his mouth and was calling to Vic, but Vic could not make out what he was saying and his words were lost, heard only by the trees.

Vic and Dave were in the orchard for just on three hours before the rain came on and then Dave took the spreader back to the machinery shed and went home. Vic unloaded the remaining bags of fertilizer and drove the ute to the far end of the orchard. He didn't want to see Jane, didn't want to hear her views on the meeting. The thought that Herbert and Edna were gone and might not be back seemed as improbable as losing the football club or closing the school or moving to Bendigo. He felt tired and the drum of the rain on the ute lulled him to sleep.

– ★ –

The desperado was in the ute, sitting in the passenger seat. Vic let out a shock of air when he saw him.

"Sleep sound as a newborn." The desperado chided. "Likely get you killed one day."

The rain had stopped but it seemed, to Vic, that his legs were near frozen. He wanted to move, to rub at his limbs but he wasn't sure what the desperado would do.

"All this thinkin' of stayin' or goin' don't make no sense." The desperado looked out the window to where the sober hills loomed in the distance. "Man orta know."

"You should go," Vic heard himself say and he felt, suddenly, that it was the desperado who was in danger and that he was the threat. The recognition of this was on his face, and the desperado, Vic saw, understood it too.

He looked up at Vic, and Vic saw the green of his eyes flecked with brown and they seemed younger, much younger than he was, as if the eyes did not belong to him at all. The desperado pushed open the door and got out. Vic watched him walk towards the settling twilight until he merged into it and Vic could not distinguish one from the other.

The ute rested next to the grandstand. It was the night before he would play the most important game of his life and Vic knew he had to try and focus. Tomorrow would be something he thought had passed him by.

If his mother were here, she would reassure him. He thought about how he used to feel watching John play in a Grand Final. He remembered how, if Henrithvale had the ascendancy, he would not move lest he disturb some cosmic force that had bestowed favour onto the Henrithvale team. In close games, he would rock and then suddenly explode with glee or anguish. The world around him disappeared; it was always just him and the game.

Vic wandered down into the clubrooms. There were balloons and streamers hanging down from the roof, and Brian had set out all the premiership cups that Henrithvale had ever won. Next to each cup was a picture of the winning team and frayed scrapbooks of newspaper articles. Those in the photos were forever linked to the cup they had won and to each other. As Vic saw the players enter the room and pause before the collection, as he had done, he knew that this was something they wanted too.

Vic sat down on the bench that lined the wall and undressed. He took his time to find the old shorts, the old jumper. He didn't want to rush anything, didn't want anything to pass too quickly, so that in days or years to come he might not be able to recall it all in detail. He watched the faces of those around him and listened to their clear voices.

Brian moved in amongst the players, and when they were all gathered, he stretched out his arms and shepherded them into a corner. This was one of Brian's many well-worn ploys, but one he reserved for those games he saw as having the potential to be transformative. They had to bunch in together so closely that there seemed to be fewer of them than there actually were. Then Brian took a chair, placed it in front of them and leaned against it as he spoke.

"Tonight," he said, so loudly that he had to take in more air, "won't be a long session. We'll do the drills that have put us in our first Grand Final in more than twenty years." He paused to let the players absorb the idea of it.

"On these tables," he pointed to the trophies and memorabilia, "are the things this club has earned and the names of those that have earned them. These are the men who didn't give in"—his voice started to build — "men who sacrificed for each other, sacrificed for their mates. Now it's your turn." He pointed at the players, at Dave, at Vic, at the others who had all seen their fathers and grandfathers achieve such greatness. "It's time for everyone here to add their names to the list!"

He went over to the table and held up a premiership cup.

"You don't get this for trying. You don't get this crossing your fingers and hoping it all works out. You get this because you're willing to do more than the bloke on the other team is willing to do. You run harder, tackle harder and give more."

Vic wanted the game to start now. He felt as if he could run straight through the walls and kick the ball a hundred metres.

"Now let's go!" Brian pointed towards the door with a clenched fist and the players bustled down the race and out into the brisk air.

The ground was washed in light. Vic jogged laps with his team mates in silence, as if in supplication. Brian instructed them to take it easy, to save it for the match but Vic could also feel the indecision in the playing group. He could sense the energy, but he also knew that nobody wanted to do anything that might strain a muscle or tear a ligament. They were so close now. It might be the last time that Henrithvale would ever field a team.

They trained for forty-five minutes, but it seemed to Vic little more than a quick kick. Afterwards, before anyone could shower, Brian assembled the team in the clubrooms and dragged over his chalkboard. Standing next to it, he talked through their game plan. It was nothing new, only now it all seemed to have significance. He pointed at players, went over targets and transitions, where to put the ball, how the forwards would set up and how the backs would set up. There were no questions or jokes from the players— not even Dave.

At the end of it, Brian seemed like he might wilt. It was as if, Vic thought, he was coming out of a trance; shedding a version of himself of which he was unaware. He pulled over a chair so that he was close to the group and sat down. The players gathered around him. When Brian began to speak it reminded Vic of being very young and hearing a teacher read some fantastical tale to the class on a drab and windy day.

"What I saw out there tonight was not passable. I would go as far to say it wouldn't win us a single game, let alone a Grand Final." Brian interlocked his reddish fingers, looking around at the players.

"Never mind. It has been a difficult few days and nowhere feels it more than a football club."

Vic felt like Brian had something more to say. His hands gripped the edges of the bench and he felt as if he had been winded, like he needed to vomit. Something was coming, something that he needed to be away from.

"Well, I have some news, a letter received this morning." Brian took the envelope out of his back pocket and, without the usual pause, began reading. "'Dear Mr Hennan, your application for a review pertaining to the ongoing viability of the Western Football League has concluded. The independent body charged with the review will inform you of its finding in coming days. And on it goes." He stuffed the letter back into his pocket.

Nobody moved. The next word could bring disaster.

"I do, however," Brian raised his voice, "have it on good authority that the Western Football League will continue to function with reduced rounds, a reduced season, and that Henrithvale will continue to be a part of that league." There was a long silence as if the words had to be carefully deciphered before they could be understood. Vic felt relief, sensed it wash through the room. Dave, sitting next to him on the bench, pushed playfully into him.

"Good on ya, Brian!" came a call and others joined in, but Brian raised his hands and called for such nonsense to end.

"Now, now," Brian said, using the back of the chair as a brace to get to his feet, "that's not all. It is important that no one leaves before we have a further discussion on a matter unrelated to football but of vital importance to Henrithvale."

Vic was the last one out of the showers, the team giving him a rowdy welcome as he finally emerged, dressed again in his everyday clothes, carrying a wet towel and dirty shorts.

Brian waited until he sat down on the bench and then he started to speak.

"This isn't news that is hot off the press, but the Henrithvale Consolidated School will be closing at the end of the year, or so says the Department of Education." He spoke in an uncharacteristically quiet voice as if delivering difficult news. "I know some of you have children at the school, have had children at the school. This is something I am not sure if I should say, but it needs to be said. I have been told, informally so, in my role as president of the Henrithvale Growers' Association that the government will rescind its demand for the compulsory requisition of irrigation leases."

Vic looked at those around him and they looked back with equal suspicion.

"Say that again, Brian?" Dave said, stunned, as he scratched at the side of his head.

"Don't get ahead of yourselves, this situation might just be temporary, and I have not heard anything else," Brian said, "but I say this to you now because it shows what people like us, people those in Canberra think can be forgotten about, can achieve when we stick together and work hard. I intend to fight for the school in the same way." Thankful applause started but was cut down by Dave.

"This better not be bullshit, Brian." Dave questioned.

"It is not official, I have not said that it is, but I have it from a very reliable source."

Players were knocking into each other, slapping each other on the back and making jokes. Vic slumped onto the bench. He let out a squeak that was part relief and part cry. Next to him Dave was scratching at his arms.

Brian hastily tried to subdue the group but could not. Vic asked Brian to repeat his statement as did others and each time Brian seemed to emphasise the doubt of what he had announced.

"I'll have a fuckin' stroke." Dave stood up, snatched his bag and marched towards the door. Vic watched him leave and despite the high mood, Brian went about packing away the equipment. If the school remained, if some version of it could hold, Vic thought, then he could put together a good reason for Jane and the girls to stay in Henrithvale at least for another year, and things might continue to turn for the better. Vic helped Brian carry footballs and lock the clubrooms. When he got out to the ute it was the only vehicle in the car park, waiting patiently and alone. He wanted to go back into the clubrooms, he wanted John to know that he too could win a premiership, could be a farmer; and if he did these things then nothing John had ever said to him would be true anymore.

— ★ —

Jane was watching TV, and there were traces of a sandalwood candle she said helped her relax. The girls were already asleep. He stood in the doorway between the kitchen and the lounge and watched Jane as she roamed the four channels on the TV. He was grinning; he couldn't help it. The football club would have another chance.

She seemed more surprised by his grin than by his sudden entrance.

"What are you so happy about?" she asked, turning her attention back to the TV and the jumbled channels.

"Brian reckons we'll be alright. He says the Greater Western Districts Football Association will reverse its decision on appeal and let the league stay. He also reckons the government will let us keep our leases." He stood behind her on the worn lounge room carpet that had been in the house longer than he had. She switched off the TV. The news did not seem to be of much interest to her.

"Brian just knows everything, doesn't he?"

"He is the—"

"I know who he is, Vic." She's too tightly wound.

He sat down on the couch and folded his hands behind his head. In the far corner of the room there was an unmoveable mark on the carpet from where, every December, the Christmas tree would be placed. It had been his mother's favourite time of the year. Vic wanted to tell her about what had happened.

"Vic." She turned to face him. "I am sick and tired of Brian Hennan. There won't be a school, Vic. Do you understand? We have kids, what are we going to do?" Here we go.

"If the water lease stays then—"

"Then what? What?"

"It's a chance, isn't it?" He needed her to say that it was a chance, that she would stick with him and they'd fight it out together.

"No, it's not. It's not. We've suffered, Vic. Now, it's Emily and Sarah, they've got to suffer so you can grow apples?"

"Please, Jane," he pleaded. He rested his elbows on his knees and held his head in his hands. It was dirty pool.

"Money will fall from the sky, will it?" She asked. He waited.

"No. No, it won't fall from the sky."

"No, it'll be just like it was. Won't it?"

"Probably."

"Only Emily and Sarah won't have a school. What are you going to do about that?" The words had a solidifying effect on the muscles in his back and across his shoulders. "I want to make a decision with you, Vic, but you just won't. I've got to do something. Look at where we're at." He closed his eyes. "All you talk about is the football club, the farm and that fucking Brian Hennan."

He had to think for a long time before he answered.

"I dunno what to say." He stammered. "When we got married, I thought—"

"When we got married the world looked very different."

"Yeah," he lamented.

"You know what I mean, Vic. We've got a chance to get out, start somewhere else."

"Some chance."

"You're a wonderful father," Jane continued. "You are. Our girls adore you. They're always asking when you'll be home, when you'll come in. They don't see enough of you."

He looked at the blank TV screen and saw a reflection of himself sitting alone.

"If you want this marriage, if you really want it, then you should do something about it," Jane said. "Stop putting it back on me." His arguments, he knew, were thin, but she didn't understand. If you stay on your feet, stay in the contest, anything can happen.

"Can we just—" She interrupted him, but he wasn't sure he had anything to add.

"I'm going Vic, I am. Emily and Sarah are coming with me and it's heartbreaking." Her voice came apart. "You do what you want."

He peeked out at her; there was nothing to say. He closed his eyes until he heard her get up and go into the bedroom and shut the door. Those words had been coming for so long it was almost a relief to hear them.

He wondered if all he was ever doing was passing time, that life was only ever a series of distractions, shifts in momentum, seen and believed as promises. For all his defiance and rage, nothing had really been achieved. What was it, he wondered, that urged him on to the unattainable? A fundamentalism mixed with naivety and foolishness. They were his failings, but he feared they did not stem from denial or stoicism, but they were innate and inevitable.

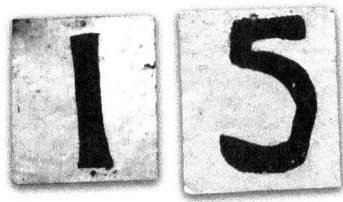

## 15

Vic woke up, hours before sunrise, from a dreamless sleep. He hadn't slept. Jane was, he decided, just letting off steam. She wouldn't go, she couldn't. His thoughts were drawn to the vegetable garden that he had planted with his mother when he was seven or eight. They turned over the earth and he held fat worms in his hands as they stretched and contracted; his mother called them Wilburs and he did the same for his girls. They planted seeds for tomatoes, basil, beetroot and corn. His mother explained that from the seed would emerge the beginnings of the plant; that it would push its way up through the earth to find the sunlight. In the days after, he woke up eager to see if the seed had taken. Once a plant had broken the surface, he measured the growth every morning.

Yet, there were some seeds that never sprouted. His mother had told him that sometimes a seed just didn't have life in it, but he didn't think that was true. He had read that some seeds can be dormant for years or decades, maybe longer; they wait until the right conditions and then life comes reaching up out of the ground. In time everything rises.

When the sun came up, Vic got out of bed and saw that the sky was a perfect and clear blue. He was ready to drive to the ground, to just sit in the clubrooms alone and let the day start.

He had three eggs and four sausages for breakfast, drinking two cups of coffee. He packed his bag, then unpacked it, checked it over, then packed it again. He was pacing in the kitchen when Jane woke up.

"Everything alright?" she asked half-heartedly, scuffling through the kitchen in worn pink slippers. No mention of leaving.

"Might head down to the ground," he said and securing his bag to his shoulder and wondering if he should go through it one more time, just in case he had missed something.

Her eyes checked the clock above the oven.

"Now? Bit early?"

"Might just see what's goin' on." She reached over to the kettle and took some bread out of the pantry. "You thinkin' of comin'?"

She frowned at him.

"Vic, I know this is important to you. The girls know it's important to you."

"Alright." He was relieved. "I'll see you there?"

"Good luck." She leaned forward and kissed him on the cheek.

Vic made his way quickly to the ute, chased by a nagging feeling that the ground was no longer fifteen minutes away. He reversed the ute out of the carport and knocked over the rubbish bin. He thought about leaving it but decided that it could foreshadow defeat, so he got out and straightened it before driving towards the road.

When he got into town there were maroon and blue streamers and balloons tied around every telephone pole, every street light. He turned onto the gravel driveway that led down to the oval and parked the ute beside the grandstand, where a dozen other cars were already waiting. Doc, Dave, the Pattison boys and some others had congregated nearby, having already made the pilgrimage. Vic went through his bag one last time, tried to get out of the ute before he had taken off his seatbelt, and then finally clambered out and approached the group.

"A bit fuckin' late," Dave smirked. He was clean shaved, his hair neatly combed.

"Couldn't sleep."

"You are not alone there," Doc answered. In the still morning their breath came out in white puffs.

"Where's Brian?" Vic asked.

"His car is here, but I haven't seen him yet." Doc was leaning against the sandstone bricks of the Henrithvale Town Stand.

"Seen the paper?" Dave handed Vic a copy of a city paper. The headline read: "Dam Damned—Towns Saved." In all the years he had known Dave, he had never seen him with a newspaper.

"Read the fuckin' fine print on page five," Dave added. He no longer seemed carefree and ready for the game. Vic put his bag down and turned the difficult broadsheet to page five.

"Here. Start right here," Dave tapped on the article with his finger. "Read that."

Vic read out loud:

"'Although the requisition of water leases from farmers in the Henrithvale district will no longer be compulsory, Minister for the Environment, Warren Evans, said the Government was still determined to return water to the Sterling River catchment and improve the health of the river system. 'The offers sent to farmers earlier this year are still alive. It is crucial to the long-term survival of rural Victoria that there be an available and dependable flow of water through this river system.'"

Vic stopped. It wasn't anything they didn't already know.

"Keep goin'," Dave insisted.

Half-heartedly, Vic read on:

"'Evans was non-committal on exactly how this would be achieved without the compulsory requisition of leases, saying, 'We are currently reviewing the structure of all existing water leases that are connected to the Sterling River system, and it may mean a change in the structure of some leases.' It is expected government will announce a reduction in the allocation each farmer receives, with future allocations also to be based on viable acreage and projected sales.'"

The article went on, but Vic stopped reading.

"See!" Dave demanded.

"Fuck that." Vic could clearly see what was written between the lines. "Viable acreage and projected sales," he said with contempt. "They'll get us anyway; kill us off one by one." Vic handed the paper back to Dave.

"Yeah," Dave spat and screwed the paper into a ball and threw it into a nearby bin. "Fuck Brian." It was rare for Dave to be angered, it made people tense. "Should've kept his fuckin' mouth shut."

"Well boys," Doc said, stretching his long arms out so they touched the shoulders of those around him. "We've got a football game to win."

"Fuckin oath." Dave responded in a strong voice, changing his focus and then giving Doc a playful prod.

Brian Hennan emerged from behind the corner of the stand, hunched, tired and surprised to see so many players here so early. His neck had red blotches of shaving rash and a splash of cologne long past its date of expiry. His familiar light-blue shirt had been washed and ironed, his shoes polished so the brown leather shined.

"The protocol, for those of you who do not remember, is that players arrive ninety minutes before the game. By my watch," he didn't take his eyes off the group, "there is still the better part of four hours before the game is to commence."

"No one could sleep, Brian." Doc answered. Brian grimaced.

"I encourage you all to go home and sleep for a few hours lest you are found wanting at game's end." He put his hands on his waist and reconsidered. "Alternatively, there is plenty to be done here, and those of you wanting to occupy your time need look no further than me for guidance."

Doc went to nap in his car, while the Pattison boys and others sat aimlessly in the stand, looking as if the game had already been played and they had arrived too late to do anything but mourn its passing. Vic and Dave painted lines on the oval, tracing over what had been done in previous weeks. The morning was tinged with spring and the grass felt fresh and easy under foot. Brian appeared regularly to make sure Vic and Dave were performing the task in a way he felt appropriate.

"Reckon the old Clock'll manage?" Dave asked.

"He's the only one that's done it before," Vic said, keeping his eyes down to make sure the lines were perfect.

Steadily, people arrived and the crowd grew. After Vic and Dave completed the markings, they carried boxes of frozen food into the tuck shop, set up the witches' hats to structure parking and practiced kicking for goal while they ate lunch. Soon Brian called at them to go down into the clubrooms. There was less than two hours before the game was to start, but most of the team had already arrived and were in their gear; just seeing others in the Maroons' jumper made Vic feel like he was being left behind. He immediately got changed.

While Doc applied strapping, others generously applied the infamous pre-game ointment. Vic sat on the bench and held a football between his hands; hoping that this game would be the one where everything just fell into place as he always believed it would.

He felt all those different versions of himself from all those different seasons were looking at him now and saying,

"You are the one. You are here because of us and you must do this for all of us."

When the desire to start the game became too much, Vic started to pace, deliberately bumping into his team mates, reassuring them and at the same time being reassured. Above, he could hear the stand filling, the sounds filtering down into the rooms. He kept pacing, telling himself that there was nothing else to think about now, just this game. He told himself he owed it to the club, to his mother, to Dave, to his team mates, but most importantly he owed it to himself.

Half an hour before the game, Brian came into the rooms and called the players together. Peter Weston, their regular umpire, came in to the clubrooms to wish them luck and Vic could see how sombre he was. No doubt, Vic thought, he wanted to be in a Henrithvale jumper. When Peter left, Brian, looking as if the game had already been played and the outcome decided, gathered the players around him. Vic bunched in with his team mates, their arms instinctively finding each other and pulling each other closer.

"Now, despite what you might think," Brian began, an unusual lethargy tugging at his words, "despite what you might well be expecting, this isn't the time for grandiose words or emotion." Brian removed his glasses and brushed his hair across his forehead. "Some of you may well know that I've done this a few times as a player, and I can tell you that getting yourself all fired up is not the way to go about it. You've got a job; we've got a job. We're going to finish what we've started."

"Those blokes next door," he pointed in the direction of the opposition change rooms, "they are thinking the same as you. In a few minutes we'll go out on the ground, get a feel for it, get a feel for the ball, look and listen. No doubt many of you will have never played in front of a mob of this size, but you need to switch it off. Your focus is quarter one."

He clumsily took the square chalkboard off the wall. As he began to go over starting positions and what was expected, Vic could feel and then hear the blood in the veins of those around him; the tremors in their arms and legs as their hearts beat. The heat rub ointment had been so liberally applied that Vic could taste it in the air, and it made his eyes water. Brian finished by pounding his right hand hard against the chalkboard.

"Alright, out we go," he said, leading Vic and the rest of the team towards the door.

Vic pushed up close behind Doc in the race, running on the spot. The light at the end of the race was hidden by the players in front of him. The ointment vapours were condensed, he swooned, and his arms felt like they held some great weight. As he began to move down the race, streaks of light cut through the black and a roll of noise reverberated so loudly that it came through the brick walls, circled behind him and compelled him forwards. He could not feel his legs, but he knew that they were still moving; then he breached the race and came out into the day. A great bombardment of indistinguishable voices, car horns, and some version of the club song on the public address, propelled him into the sky so that he felt nothing but sound.

As he touched the field he turned and saw that the Henrithvale Town Stand was overflowing. Supporters began singing the Maroons' theme song. Vic felt as if he could not take in enough air.

"Fuck me," he heard Dave gasp.

Brian's voice was fuzzy, calling on the players to stretch and move the balls through a warmup rotation. Players fumbled and miskicked, and Brian again yelled at them to calm down and focus.

A section of the stand cheered as the North West team came out onto the ground. They were relatively new to the league, having joined in 1960 when the town, which had thrived on gold during the nineteenth century and then all but disappeared in the Great Depression, was reborn with new mines in the post-World War II era. They wore a black jumper with a yellow sash running from top left to bottom right. They had been the dominant force in the league in recent years, but this season they had been weakened with teams in other leagues having poached their better players.

Vic stretched his legs as the feeling in them returned and then Brian's voice became clearer.

"In! In!" Brian moved his arms as if he were scooping the players up. "Listen! Those blokes over there," he pointed in the direction of the North West Tigers, "they've done this before. They'll come out hard. Keep your feet, don't drop your head and your time will come." His glasses were off again, and he fixed his eyes on Vic.

"Don't leave this ground without a win."

Brian led the players over to the area of the ground in front of the Henrithvale Town Stand. They stood in a line, shoulder to shoulder, facing the North West Tigers as a tired version of the Australian national anthem clogged the public address system. There was silence through the first verse and into the chorus, but then, no longer willing to wait, the crowd erupted into cheers. Vic wouldn't have known the song was finished if it hadn't been for the players around him moving into a huddle.

Dave ran away from the group and into the centre to meet with Peter Weston, and the Captain of the North West Tigers. They shook hands and Peter Weston flipped a coin in the air. It landed and then Dave pointed towards the end of the ground closest to the Royal Mail Hotel. Dave jogged back to the huddle and thrust himself into the middle.

"Our whole fuckin' lives we've been waitin' for this." He sounded angry, cheated and Vic felt it too. "Let's fuckin' do it," his voice boiled. "C'mon!" The players broke from the huddle and ran to position, crossing in front of and behind the North West players.

Vic found his way to the forward pocket and his opponent, a tall solid man, immediately dug a knuckle into Vic's ribs.

"You're fucked," the man goaded with his head down, his black hair parted on one side. Vic shoved him away and jogged forward, but he stuck close. "You need to lose some weight, mate? Looks like you're pregnant." Vic ignored him for now, just wanted the ball in his hands.

The siren sounded. Peter Weston blew his whistle, held the ball in the air, and the game began.

The ball was slammed down into the ground and soared high and straight. It held against the blue of the sky and was then smothered by a crash of players and the raucousness of the stand. Vic couldn't make out what was happening. Then he heard the whistle and saw a Tigers player emerge with the free kick. Henrithvale players ran to fill up space on the ground, but the Tigers player was precise, and his kick hit a tall leading forward who had cut his way through the defence. The forward took his time, jogged in and kicked the first goal of the game. His North West team mates ran from all over the ground to congratulate him, pushing and knocking into Henrithvale players as they went.

Peter Weston again sent the ball up and Dave quickly emerged from the pack, looking for a forward option, but before he could kick, he was run down from behind and tackled. The Tigers player was rewarded with a free kick and pushed the ball across to the open space on the other side of the ground. There was a Tigers loose player; he found the ball, touched it on the ground and easily kicked the second goal of the game. Again, the Tigers celebrated.

"Too easy, Tiges!" Someone yelled.

Vic felt nauseous. Panic was coming to life inside him. Henrithvale couldn't keep up with the pace of the game. The ball was again sent up straight and this time Adam Pattison jumped over the top of the Tigers ruckman, punching the ball twenty metres towards the Henrithvale goal. Vic led out wide creating room for Doc, but Dean Pattison got hands on the ball and was then driven into the ground earning a free kick. Dave pulled the offending Tigers player off Dean and was then knocked to the ground himself. Peter Weston blew his whistle.

"I warned you before the game," he said. "Fifty metre penalty."

It put Dean right in front of goal, and he kicked Henrithvale's first. Now it was Henrithvale's turn to celebrate. Vic grasped Dean's shoulders, but he longed to touch the ball, just for a moment.

The pace of the game slowed so that it became a contest between half-back lines, each preventing the ball from finding its way into the hands of the opposition forwards. Vic could sense the strain on the Henrithvale side and soon their backline could not clear the ball past the centre. The Tigers pushed harder, their tackling was relentless and soon Henrithvale had given up three more goals. Vic still hadn't touched the ball. The Tigers pressed forward again, but the siren sounded to end the quarter.

As the Henrithvale players made their way to the quarter time huddle, Vic could hear the loud voices of the Tigers players, urging each other on. The stand sounded like the chorus from an ancient play, voicing the doubts of the Henrithvale team.

Brian had the players gather in close.

"The first quarter is gone, over and done with, but this second quarter belongs to us. Too often we drop our heads and don't take the risks we need to take." Vic was as clean as he was at the start of the game. "Listen to me. Listen!" Brian's voice exploded in their faces. "You won't win this game if you don't try. Take a stand, and if you're going to lose, then go down swinging."

Vic could feel the heat and sweat on those that brushed against him.

Brian started to call out position changes. Vic felt it coming. Brian took Adam Pattison out of the ruck and put Dean in so that he could use his body to block the Tigers ruck. Adam Pattison went to centre-half back, and Doc went to full-forward. Then Brian reached forward and grabbed Vic by the neck of his jumper, pulling him off balance.

"Get your hands on the ball!" He yelled and shoved Vic away.

Vic was too stunned to respond. The players from both teams ran back to position. The quarter started and the Tigers cleared the ball with a succession of quick handpasses and kicked a goal inside thirty seconds. The voices of the Tigers players changed— they spoke of an inevitability.

Vic's opponent clapped his hands.

"Let's smash 'em, Tiges," he called out to his team mates, and the phrase was carried around the ground.

Vic felt the need to get away, the desire to start the whole thing over again. He had to do something. He sprinted up to the wing as Peter Weston restarted play, and then he ran head down into the huddle of players who were trying to work the ball to an advantage. The huddle caved in and Dave emerged, running parallel to the goals. He handballed over the head of an approaching tackler, collected the ball again and the defenders stayed off him, trying to corral him instead. Dave stopped, circled backwards and put the ball up high. Doc caught it and slotted through Henrithvale's second goal.

Dave stopped next to Vic as he ran back to the centre.

"What the fuck were ya doin'? Ya just about killed me." Vic could not answer. Dave slapped him on the chest, "Do it again."

Vic returned to the wing, his opponent alongside him, keeping his forearm against Vic's shoulder. As soon as the ball hit the ground Vic ran straight at the pack of players again, but stopped short, pivoting so that he was suddenly behind his opponent. From there he shoved him in the back as hard as he could, straight into the oncoming melee. Peter Weston didn't see it, didn't want to. Vic's opponent picked himself up, ran back to Vic and pushed an open hand into his face. Peter Weston blew his whistle, and Vic won a free kick.

"Thanks, fuckhead." Dave patted Vic's opponent on the head as he ran past.

There was no time to think. Vic kicked the ball across the ground to where Adam Pattison had run into space. Adam marked the ball, kept running and kicked a fifty-five metre drop-punt goal.

"Yes!" Vic called out and punched his fist into the air. He felt himself, like the other Henrithvale players, peeling off a cumbersome skin and becoming taller, stronger. He understood now that there was a price to pay and there must be a willingness to do whatever was necessary to win

"Now or fuckin' never!" Dave screamed at Vic and Doc as he ran back to the centre.

Henrithvale started to claw their way back into the game, kicking two more goals and holding the Tigers to four points. At half-time Henrithvale were only ten points behind and Vic knew that they would not break. The players jogged off the ground towards the clubrooms, the stand offering an incantation to guide the team home.

In the clubrooms Vic drank some water, stretched and chewed on sugar lollies. The players called to each other, offering encouragement. Brian moved among them, rubbing his hands together. Vic's head was clear. He understood what it was he had to do; find the ball, move the ball forward, sacrifice for the team.

Eventually Brian pulled the players in so that they were around him, almost standing over him like a fortress.

"They've thrown everything at us and you know what? You know what? It wasn't enough!" Vic called to his team mates and heard it given back. "Now we're going to give them everything we've got, and they don't have a chance. Not a chance!"

As the players took to the field they were received with fanatical, hoarse voices. Vic could feel it: they would win this quarter, the Tigers would break and the last quarter would be a time to savour.

Vic found himself against a different opponent, a short stocky man around his age. Before the quarter started, he was already pushing into Vic and trying to block his run. When Peter Weston bounced the ball to begin the third quarter, the huddle of players moved in and then suddenly stopped.

Vic tried to run, was blocked again by his opponent but pushed him away and jogged into the centre square. Peter Weston called for the stretcher, simultaneously separating players from both teams. Adam and Dean Pattison had hold of the Tigers player who had been Vic's opponent in the first half, and they in turn had several Tigers players trying to pull them away. As more players joined, it became a scrum.

Dave was on the ground, flat on his back, his arms stiff and his eyes half open. Vic had seen it before and knew that he must have been unconscious before he hit the ground.

Vic came in at the side of the huddle, jumped and grabbed a handful of the hair of the Tigers player the Pattison boys were after. Other Tigers players turned on Vic and the scrum collapsed. Vic threw wild punches without looking, but did not land anything.

Peter Weston's whistle overcame the chaos.

"Separate now or I'll call the whole fuckin' game off!"

By the time they had separated, Dave was awake. The trainers were putting a neck brace on him. Adam Pattison was hunched nearby, his hands covering the right side of his face. Nobody saw what happened. Doc kneeled beside him and pried away his hands. The right side of Adam's face was bulging and his eye was swollen shut.

"Awww." Doc looked up at Vic. "It's his jaw."

The trainers secured Dave to a stretcher, and to kind appreciation from the stand, carried him from the ground. Adam Pattison, leaning on a Tigers trainer, was behind him. The Henrithvale players came together and waited.

"We'll just keep doin' what we're doin'." Vic's timid voice implored as he searched for Brian who was standing near the boundary line waving directions.

Brian sent runners out from the bench to swing players and cover the gaps. Vic's gaze turned to the cornered blue sky above as it was besieged by a voracious and ashen stormfront; a light shower started to fall. The Henrithvale structures seemed exposed now and Vic wasn't sure what he should do.

The North West players seemed far more self-assured now. Vic could see the change in their body language. When Peter Weston blew the whistle to recommence play the Tigers took control of the game, keeping Henrithvale from scoring and adding four goals and five points of their own. It would have been more, but the ball had become greasy with the rain. The stand was mute.

Vic was loitering in the centre of the churned ground with his hands on his hips. The game was escaping him and he did not know how to get it back. As the ball went out of bounds, he was taken by the size of the Henrithvale Town Stand. He had sat there so many times in his life. Now those people watched him and wanted him to be the one who could win the game. Above, more of the blackening clouds were being siphoned into the valley, bringing with them the promise of a calamitous rain.

Vic heard the sound of the ball being kicked, the perfect sound as it left the boot and turned through the air. The ball landed twenty metres away from him, but he was behind his opponent and had to give chase. Vic made up the ground and was able to push and claw his opponent and the ball out of play.

"Well done, Vic." The call came from over the fence and he stopped at the impossible familiarity of the voice. He ignored the game and searched the faces in the crowd; it was his mother's voice, he was sure of it.

"C'mon, Vic," Doc urged, as the boundary umpire hoisted the ball back into play.

"Go on, Vic, you can do it." Vic knew it was her, but he did as she asked and started running. The ball was forward of him now, and he ran to catch up to the pack that was hunting it. Players from both teams dived on the ball to try and lock it in, but there was a Henrithvale player he didn't recognise bullocking his way to the front, head over the ball. As the player made his way forward, he suddenly stopped and handballed the ball out to Vic, some twenty metres to the left of the congestion.

Vic had ten metres on his opponent, with the goals fifty metres away. He couldn't kick that far on a dry day and now the ball was waterlogged. He ran, reaching down to touch the ball on the ground. He saw that he still had five metres on his opponent and kept moving. There was no one to pass the ball to. He looked towards the goals, with the sound of blood in his ears, and kicked. He struck the ball so that it turned and twisted —a mongrel punt Herbert would call it—but it carried the distance and gave Henrithvale their only goal of the quarter.

The celebration on the ground and in the stands was subdued, but Vic felt as if he had opened a door that had always been closed.

Less than a minute later the siren ended the quarter and the Henrithvale players trudged over to the area of the ground in front of the stand. Tigers players ran past, their bodies revealing a confidence Henrithvale could not find. As the Henrithvale team came together, the rain became thunderous, almost white. Yet the supporters did not seek shelter, stoic and defiant they stayed out in the open along the boundary fence. Brian cowered under a tattered brown raincoat and the players circled around him.

The goal had given Vic courage, but he sensed for many of his team mates the game was already lost. They would not be duped anymore.

Brian considered them as if he did not know who they were.

"This is not something I wanted to say, not today anyway. But if you need inspiration, this is as good, as tough, as it gets." Vic dropped his head. Brian's shoes and the bottom of his pants were saturated, covered in flecks of mud; and Vic felt they were no longer on the football field.

"Our appeal… our appeal to the GWDFA has failed; there is no further course of action to be taken. After today there will be no more Western Football League, there will be no more Henrithvale Football Club." Brian put his hand to his mouth. "You're it." With that the players parted and let him hobble off the ground.

No one moved. The players exchanged stares, each seeking some kind of surety from the others. Vic wanted it to be another Brian Hennan ruse, but it struck him as undeniably true. Thunder unravelled in elongated and doleful reverberations. The air felt hot in Vic's lungs and he held it there. It was now an all-or-nothing game. He had the sense that he was alone, that all the Henrithvale players were alone; and in this tempest they must now sail for home or let the mast break and hull fill with water and be damned. There was nothing in-between.

Just then, Dave emerged from the bleak, pushing his way into the huddle.

"Anyone else have a fuckin' cunt of a headache?" He asked, his eyes bloodshot. Vic was relieved to see him. Dave took charge. "I'll sit in the forward pocket. Just pump the fuckin' ball in; don't worry about kickin' it to a lead."

The siren sounded for the commencement of the last quarter.

"C'mon!" Dave raised his voice over the howl of the squall. "We'll have a fuckin' cry later." Dave reached out his arms. Vic and the team pressed in tight, nobody spoke, and then they broke away to run back to their positions.

Peter Weston blew his whistle and threw the ball in the air. Neither ruckman could get a decisive knock, but a Henrithvale player slapped the ball forward and Doc kicked it along the ground. Vic's opponent was in front of him, but fumbled, skidded, and lost his footing. Suddenly, Vic had the ball up and without looking kicked it in the general direction of the goals. Dave watched the ball in flight, blocked his opponent from the space where it was going to land, then jumped forward and marked it on his chest. He went back from the mark, calmed himself, and then kicked the opening goal of the quarter. Vic and the other Henrithvale players ran towards him.

"Five fuckin' more and it's ours!" Dave was emboldened.

"C'mon!" Vic added his voice.

The North West players were frightened. When play recommenced, Vic saw how they each wanted someone else to do the chasing, someone else to do the tackling. For five minutes the ball moved back and forth across the centre square before Peter Weston gave Doc a free kick. Doc played on and handballed to Dean Pattison, who kicked another goal. Those still in the stand pushed towards the edges of the ground, feeling that they too could decide the outcome of the match. There were no umbrellas. Vic felt their voices, brutish and ardent, invigorating.

When play restarted, the ball found its way easily into the Henrithvale forward line. Dave threw himself on top of it as the Tigers players descended. Peter Weston paid another free kick and, as the Tigers players remonstrated, Dave played on and kicked another goal. The Henrithvale players converged on Dave grabbing at his jumper, pulling at his hair. Vic could see something rising in them, coming up through the ground. They needed three goals.

The North West team moved the ball into their forward line. A player kicked wildly towards goal but missed, and Henrithvale cleared the ball up to the wing. Vic had run forward and was first to the ball; he grabbed it with both hands and was slung down hard to the muddy ground and dispossessed. There was mud in his eyes, but someone was there to help him up and to thumb the mud away. It was John, his father. He gave Vic an encouraging pat on the arm and took off towards the Henrithvale goals. Just near the fence his mother was standing with Herbert and Edna, and Jane and the girls; they held on to each other, enthralled.

Vic ran after John, but was unable to keep up. John swiftly manoeuvred himself between players and took possession of the ball. Vic kept moving towards goals. John seemed to know just where Vic would be and he kicked the ball across his body, hitting Vic on the chest. The ball was a brick and Vic could barely keep hold of it. He played on and kept running, his lungs too shocked to take in air, and kicked, watching the ball as it skated through for another goal. He pumped his fist in the air as the Henrithvale players mobbed him, the torrential rain forming vast puddles on the ground.

Twice Henrithvale moved the ball forward; twice they kicked for goal and missed. They were eight points behind and still needed two goals. The quarter was more than twenty minutes old; there could be no more than five minutes left.

Dave ran past Vic and said he was moving into the centre. Vic stayed across the half-forward line. Dave took the ball from the centre and kicked long into the forward line. The ball fell through fingers and hit the muddy ground, players from both teams converged.

"Hold it in! Hold it in!" The Tigers yelled at each other.

Peter Weston blew his whistle and then threw the ball in the air to restart play. John ran in-between the two competing ruckmen, grabbed the ball and kicked, without even setting foot on the ground. The ball, like a great weight, beat the outstretched hands of the Tigers defenders and sailed through for another goal. Henrithvale players threw their arms in the air in wild elation. They embraced Vic and patted him on the head.

One more goal and the game was theirs. The shouts of the true believers subdued the storm and told Vic the game could be won.

The Tigers were broken. As Peter Weston restarted play there were too many Tigers players in the centre square. Dean Pattison took the free kick and drove the ball forward. Doc took a juggling chest mark in the middle of a group of six players. The Henrithvale faithful, ecstatic and uninhibited, seemed like they might rush onto the ground. Doc took a breath and kicked. Vic watched as the ball was signalled a goal and then the scoreboard was adjusted to show Henrithvale in front by four points.

"We've gotta hold on now!" Dave screamed at them.

Peter Weston looked up at the sky, cleaned the ball with his shirt as if stalling, and then restarted play. The ball moved into the Henrithvale forward line but was quickly cleared out again with two handpasses then a barrelling torpedo that sent it into the Tigers forward line. Peter Weston blew his whistle; there was a mark, but

Vic couldn't see for which team. His heart slowed to a painful thud, then floated to the surface of his skin. It was a Tigers forward. Vic waited as the forward positioned himself, then kicked the ball. It looked a certain goal, but the wind tossed it about and it seemed to have gone left. The goal umpire dithered, then signalled a goal. The Tigers players leapt in the air, ecstatic; they were back in front.

"Still a chance, Vic. Just one more," Dave urged, as he ran into the middle for the restart. He wasn't beaten, but Vic felt sick. He waited just outside the centre square. When the ball came out, it moved towards the Tigers goal. The Tigers players pushed up the ground, trying to lock the ball in their forward half and the Henrithvale players followed them. Vic stood back waiting fifty metres from the Henrithvale goal.

Then he saw John pushing through a pack of players, accelerating away, carrying the ball and avoiding outstretched arms. He ran directly towards Vic, through the centre of the ground. Vic ran back towards the Henrithvale goal, leaving his opponent caught between him and John. There were Tigers players chasing John but they weren't gaining on him. Vic was only thirty metres away from the Henrithvale goal and his opponent had left him and was running to block John. John kicked the ball high into the air, and Vic watched it turn through the sky like a shooting star falling to earth. The ball carried over Vic's head. He ran to catch it before it hit the ground. There was nothing between him and the goal. He reached out his hands, the ball scraped his fingertips, but it was just beyond him; his calf muscles strained and constricted. He needed the ball to sit up so he could run on to it; but it hit the sodden ground and took a low, sharp break to the left. He stretched out his left hand, his fingertips brushing the ball's rough surface again, but it escaped him. A pursuing Tigers player hurriedly kicked it back the way it had come.

Vic lunged to affect the kick, but he was too late. The siren sounded. The game was over.

The Tigers players were jubilant. Vic felt as if he were spinning around and around, end over end. He needed more time but fell back onto the ground and the blustering rain berated him. He sat up and pulled his jumper half over his head and cried, great and terrible cries that had lain dormant within him for decades, and he could not stop. Someone rubbed his head.

"Unlucky bounce, mate." It was Dave, who dropped down next to him and wrapped his arms around Vic's shoulders, kissing the top of his head. Vic clung to him.

Others came over to them, some rubbing Vic's head, others crying. In time they helped each other to their feet and trudged towards the clubrooms. Dave kept an arm around Vic's shoulders. Tradition demanded that Henrithvale stay on the ground until after the presentation of the premiership cup, but it did not matter any longer. As the Henrithvale team approached the stand the solemn congregation with their heads bowed, parted, but they too were broken, they too had been deceived yet again. Vic heard the click of his boots on the concrete of the race and felt the ground telling them to leave.

Brian wouldn't let anyone but the players in the clubrooms. He locked the door and they sat together in a silence that would bind them to each other forever. Now Vic could feel the stinging cuts and the fatigued muscles, it was the best game he had ever played and the worst he had ever felt. He looked quickly at his father's photo on the wall above. The old man had been right about him. Vic took his towel out of his bag and hung it over his head. Nobody said anything for a long time. Some around him started to rise, move into the showers and dress, but Vic stayed where he was. He listened to the sound of them moving, of their bags opening. The showers made the air muggy and he knew there was no such thing as redemption.

Vic knew that Brian was close; dragging that pained and useless leg of his around the room. Vic stood up, collected his things and went into the showers. He didn't wash, just stood under the shower head, hiding in the vapours. Eventually, long after the water had turned cold, he dressed and looked at his muddy jumper, discarded on the bench. It was never much to look at, but it made him better than he ever was or ever would be.

With the players back in their everyday clothes, Brian cleared his throat loudly to get their attention. He seemed about to speak, but his face flushed with emotion and he tilted his head towards the photos and trophies that lined the walls.

"We tried...." It was all he could say and then he turned his back on the group, but they came to him and embraced him. For a second, he embraced them too.

"Alright. Alright." Brian adjusted his tie and glasses, tucked in his shirt, and then went down the race. He opened the door; wives, brothers, children and friends filled the room, found their loved ones and hugged them, held their hands, commiserated.

Vic couldn't bring himself to look for Jane and the girls. With his head down, he became an echo that scurried out of the clubrooms and into the hopelessness of the late afternoon. The rain was gone. There had been plans to gather at the Royal Mail for post-match drinks, but Vic wanted no part of it and he guessed that neither did anyone else.

Jane and the girls would be here somewhere, but when the weather was like this Jane stayed in the car. So be it. He could not look at his team mates or the stand or the ground or the people around him. He had failed them, but they had failed him too. To look at Dave or Doc or Brian, to walk out on the ground and be where he had come so close to absolution was not a weight he could carry. It was a grief akin to that he felt when his mother died, that he still felt when he thought about her for too long. Today there had been the chance to act. He thought of himself sinking and then settling on the ocean floor like the wreck of some great ship.

He got in the ute and sobbed, keeping his head down lest he be seen. He drove away from the ground and away from the town. He found himself turning down a gravel road and stopping in the car park of the Henrithvale cemetery.

The cemetery was serene, surrounded by rugged hills. There were two sections: one for before 1930 and one for after 1930. Most of the graves in the old section were unmarked, the fires from 1930 burnt through the cemetery and few markers were replaced.

Vic's mother and John were buried next to each other in the bottom left corner of the new section, although it was his mother's grave that marked the bottom corner. Vic had been at her graveside when she was interred and again when John was buried, but he had never thought of her as being in this place, so far away from where she should be. Her grey stone marker had her name, date of birth and date of death, but those things, Vic thought, didn't say anything about her at all.

The grass was cut short, and he sat down next to her and shared the view of the hills that were now all but lost in the shapeless evening; he felt the damp ground coming through his pants.

There were things he wanted to say, so that she knew, so that she understood, but they could not be said with words. The crickets started to call in the night. Maybe tomorrow, he thought. He stood up, his arms stiff, and put his left hand lightly on her gravestone. He went quickly back to the ute and drove towards home along the roads that had carried him his entire life.

# 16

The rain returned and Vic, his hips and knees stiffening from the game, steered the ute back towards town. As he neared the turn for the main road through town, he pushed on the brakes and pulled onto the shoulder of the road. A thin whistle of wind forced its way in through the frayed door seals. The rain was gone, and the night was unfathomable. In the distance he could see the street light near Jack and Edna's store. Someone was standing underneath it, a silhouette that he squinted at as the ute's windscreen began to fog. The figure under the streetlight seemed to have sensed him. Vic opened the door of the ute and the interior light caught and then disappeared when he climbed out and shut the door. He braced for a desolate cold, for a shiver to run across his shoulders, but it didn't come. Instead he found the pungent excesses of summer; the sun-hardened ground and a tepidness nourished by the rain. As he approached the figure under the street light, a yawning wind rushed through him, and he waited until it had gone. As he got closer to the streetlight, he could see the figure in more detail. It was Mulholland.

"Ah Vic, I knew you'd come. And what a fine night it is." His hands together as if in prayer and his voice had an ugly eagerness in it. "Now, it was a hard day, but what a triumph!" Vic wasn't sure what he was getting at; they had lost the game and lost the football club. The irrigation leases. Bastard.

"You saw the papers. They'll still get us," Mulholland's voice became paternalistic.

"Yes, Vic, they will. But you can see it; you understand it now, don't you?" He didn't give Vic time to respond. "We won't just go away and leave you alone. We'll reduce your irrigation quota year after year, reduce your subsidy, reduce the tariffs. Starve you out and leave you with nothing." Vic heard the scuff of boots coming from the direction of the Royal Mail. He turned his head to look. There were other blinking street lights, so positioned that the light from one was separated from the next by a vast and impenetrable unknown. Mulholland hopped off the curb and came towards Vic.

"C'mon lad," Mulholland encouraged. "You can sell, Vic, right here and now, walk away with money in your pocket for yourself, for Jane and little Sarah and Emily." Mulholland reached inside his coat and withdrew a collection of documents. An abiding sincerity came into in his voice "Here it is, Vic, something for the future." Then, he understood. The desperado was close. Vic knew it too and he felt like he was reaching out for that tumbling football again. This was the future, this was progress. Like the coming and going of the seasons it didn't care about him.

"Tomorrow, Vic, the offer will be gone." Mulholland tilted his head just so. "Property prices these days are a volatile thing. If you don't take an opportunity when it comes, why it might just pass you by." Mulholland held the documents out for Vic to take. "Do you want to stay on that land without the water, without income, with your football team, and your family gone?" He imbedded the words into Vic, but those footsteps; the desperado was coming, and he needed Vic's help.

"Wait," Vic said and turned away from Mulholland and went towards where the desperado waited.

"Don't be a fool, Vic." Mulholland called after him, but Vic kept on until Mulholland was an indistinct silhouette and then he was gone altogether; Vic sensed there were others aside from the desperado watching him. He stopped in the middle of the road. The desperado emerged from a nearby laneway, passed through the benign glow of a street light and stood before Vic. They eyed each other.

"S'mthin' wrong with yer legs?" The desperado broke the silence. "Had a brother with polio move faster." The desperado held his Winchester out to Vic and Vic felt the ground open. His thoughts pitched backwards. "Go on. Take it!" The desperado thrust the rifle at him. "Y'all been starin' at it so damn long, didn't think I'd have ta get to beggin'." Vic took the rifle. The smooth buttstock and the cool metal of the octagonal barrel were reassuring.

"You gotta circle aroun', come up from the alley and get to the other side. You wait 'till I get close, wait 'till he reaches." Vic thought about his mother, about his grandfather and Jack and Edna and his girls, all watching him. "Go on!" Vic didn't move. "This is how it is. You do the choosin' or it's done for you! This is my choosin', yours too." They were just shapes, old ghosts.

"We could…" Vic began, knowing there was nothing to be said, but the desperado shoved at him, and when he tried to speak again the desperado shoved harder. He swallowed, said nothing, and reluctantly stalked off the road, between the street lights and down a side street. The dryness in his throat remained. He crossed the road behind Mulholland and looped around so he was standing a short distance from the ute. He watched as the desperado stopped at the outskirts of Jack and Edna's street light.

"Come closer where I can see you," the desperado called to Mulholland and Mulholland moved forward. Vic's eyes danced from one to the other and then back.

"This way of doing things, Vic," Mulholland gestured with a nod of his head to the desperado, "this way is in the past."

The desperado pulled his Colt .45 from its holster and pointed it at Mulholland. Mulholland, holding the documents in his left hand, began reaching inside his jacket with his right hand.

"This time right between the eyes," The desperado called. Vic pushed the curved buttstock into his shoulder, looked down the barrel in a way that was instinctive and long-practiced and squeezed the trigger. His shoulder jarred.

The desperado faltered, sank to his knees, stood up and fell back to the ground. Vic could sense shapes moving about beyond the surface. He dropped the rifle and felt the heat from the flames as he tried to salvage something of his mother from the fire his father wrought. His mouth filled with saliva, he wheeled and stumbled towards the desperado, but Mulholland stopped him.

"There we go, Vic, easy does it, easy does it." He then took a silver pen out of the breast pocket of his jacket and held it out to Vic, pointing to the line on the document where Vic needed to sign.

Vic's fingers tentatively gripped at the pen and he signed his name and then pushed away from Mulholland and collapsed next to the desperado. The desperado's shirt, where the bullet had entered his chest, smouldered. Vic patted at it with his hands. The desperado seemed to be trying to get to his feet and take in gulping breaths, but he could do neither. The heels of his boots and his fingers clawed at the ground. His shirt was turning red as the blood escaped his chest wound.

Vic pulled off his own shirt and bunched it over the desperado's wound. With his left hand he cradled the desperado's head. The desperado's hands touched at the wound and then pushed at Vic's stomach and chest. He turned his head to the left and the right to avoid looking at Vic.

"Don't..." The desperado coughed as his chest sank. "Don't you bury me in this goddamned place."

"I'm sorry." Vic could think of nothing else to say. He pressed down on his shirt and raised the desperado's head so that it lay almost in his lap.

"You ain't...you." The desperado twisted and spluttered blood at Vic and Vic instinctively lifted him up, so his legs and head were lolling over Vic's arms; together they limped back to the ute and Vic put the desperado in the passenger seat. He drove recklessly back towards the farm as the rain returned and blurred the windscreen. The moon was hidden somewhere in the night and as the ute rounded the corner towards the farm, the ute's headlights were cast out towards his father's tree. The back wheels lost traction and the ute skidded off the road and into a ditch.

Vic scrambled out of the ute, gathered up the desperado as if he were a sleeping child and staggered towards the station house. He laboured over wretched ground and could not think what he had done and did not see where Mulholland went; or if those he sensed who were watching came forward when he left. Vic kept on, reeling and swaying to the weakening wheeze of the desperado.

The station house was ready; the interior partially illuminated by a kerosene lantern and a steady fire in a hearth built of river stone. Along the wall opposite the door was a single bed, the blankets turned down in readiness; just as his mother had always done for him. Vic shut the door and the flames sputtered. There was a dimness prowling the corners of the station house; primitive things stalked across the floorboards, up the walls, vanished and then reappeared.

Vic laboured over to the bed and shoved the desperado onto the mattress and then steadied himself against a wall. He watched, waiting for the desperado to open his eyes, to curse, but as simply as if he were closing a door or taking off a long-worn pair of boots, the desperado died.

The logs in the hearth collapsed, and outside Vic could hear hailstones and a vicious wind. He carefully removed the desperado's gun belt and then undressed him; folded the desperado's clothes and placed them neatly by the bed. Blood from the desperado's wound had already pooled on the mattress. Vic covered him with a blanket but did not cover his face.

There was blood on Vic's hands, its iron rawness in his mouth. His limbs had lost circulation and he could not feel his sodden shoes but knew they were there. He went towards the door as the rattling wind pushed under it with a mourning hiss. He thought to say something, but opened the station house door, resisted the desire to look back, and closed it behind him. Then he started to run, fleeing; but to where he did not know.

#

Vic was woken by the sound of Jane frantically saying his name. He felt her hands rocking his shoulders and he opened his eyes. Jane was still rocking him, but her eyes were on the bedroom door.

"Don't come in! Sarah, don't come in!" Her voice, he thought, sounded like his.

When Jane looked down at him and saw that he was awake, she sat back on the bed, her breathing short and rapid. She didn't seem to know what to make of him; her lips were moving but they weren't making any sound.

"Mummy, mummy?" Sarah's voice called. The bedroom door creaked open. Jane got up and blocked Sarah from coming in the room.

"It's alright, Sarah, Mummy will be there in a minute." Jane pushed the door closed and returned to the bed.

Vic sat up. His back was stiff and his right shoulder was tender. There was dried blood on his hands, on the sheets and smeared across his stomach like tribal markings.

"What happened to you last night? We couldn't find you. You weren't at the Royal. Dave didn't know." She was scared.

"Ute came off the road. Got stuck in a ditch." He rubbed his hands together. "Hit my nose on the steering wheel." His left hand moved to his nose, but it was not swollen or sore. "Must've crawled home."

Jane stared in disbelief taking it all in; the blood on the sheets, on his hands, spread in patterns over his naked torso by fingers she did not know.

"I'll give Dave a call, get him to bring the tractor, haul the ute out. I'm okay."

Jane stood up and had her arms wrapped around her shoulders. She was wearing jeans and a t-shirt, but her hair was unkempt as if she had just awoken. He could tell she had been biting her fingernails again; the ends of her fingers looked inflamed. Vic dropped his feet to the floor.

"I signed last night." The words were soulless.

She accepted his admission with a relieved gasp and began to cry, her eyes low, not wanting to meet his. She opened her mouth as if to speak and then quickly, silently, left the room. He thought she might have thanked him, said something conciliatory.

Vic waited by the side of the road for Dave. The foul weather from last night had passed and the sky was a placid blue. He could see the distant hills and the desperado receding into the past. Vic heard Dave before he saw him and turned to watch the tractor struggling along the road. Dave, in sleeveless overalls and muddy boots, stopped alongside Vic. He looked at the ute in the ditch.

"Shit place to park."

"Yeah, nice view though."

They got ropes under the ute and around the front-end. Then Vic started the ute and Dave urged the tractor forward. The ute came out effortlessly.

"Coulda driven it out, saved me the effort." Dave turned the tractor's engine off.

"How's ya head?" Vic asked, as he cleared debris from the grill of the ute.

"Alright," Dave said, blocking the sun from his eyes with his hands.

"Yeah," Vic stood up and dusted off his pants.

"Shit game, eh?" Dave complained.

"I reckon." Vic looked at the ground.

"So, I sold up. Reckon you have too." Dave said in a timid voice. Vic wasn't sure what to say. "Did it when the offers first come. Stayed for the footy season. Gonna go next week."

"Yeah. I'm goin' too." Vic confessed and rubbed his hands together.

"Gunna clean out that fuckin' stink shed of yours?" Dave asked.

"Probably should." Vic felt ashamed.

"They can fuckin' have all the shit I've got stuck in sheds here and there." Vic didn't know how to continue and he got the feeling that Dave didn't either.

"We're goin' ta Bairnsdale. June's got a sister who lives there. We're thinkin' of a bed-and-breakfast. Enough fuckin' farmin'. Gonna use me people skills." He reached into his pocket and took out a small piece of paper. On it, in neat capitals he had written his name and a Bairnsdale address. Awkwardly, Vic took the piece of paper from Dave.

"Yeah, no worries." He wondered how to reciprocate.

They shook hands. David Foster, the most ardent and reliable of friends. Vic could not recall an argument or harsh word between them. It was Dave who had so often been there when his mother could not, Dave who would not let him fall. Yet he could not look at Dave and not think of John or of Brian or the football club or the farm or his mother.

"Don't be a stranger," Dave winked. The tractor laboured forward, and Vic held up his right hand as Dave drove away. Then he got the ute home and sat in the carport. He could see the house and he wondered if there would be other people living in it after they had gone, or if it would be left so that in time the roof would collapse and the rain would find its way in, the walls buckling and then collapsing. Then grass seeds would get inside one day and eventually there would be just the foundations left to let show that once there was a home here.

As soon as Vic opened the back door, Jane embraced him, her hands and arms making the shape of his shoulders but hovering just above them; as if he were so brittle that an embrace might shatter him.

"Thank you. Thank you for putting your family first." She was over compensating and reminded him of a politician, an administrator. The family he had put first was her and the girls, but in doing that he turned his back on his mother.

"Well it's done now. That's it."

"Do you want to tell Emily and Sarah?" He couldn't do it, couldn't answer their questions, not truthfully.

"Nah, you do it."

"There must be a lot to sort through?" she asked.

"Yeah, too much. But not today. Might go for a walk." She was making pancakes and the butter was burning; when she turned back to them, he left.

He wandered over to the machinery shed and stood inside. There was too much to sort through. He had no idea what might be buried under the boxes and engine parts and tools that had accumulated generation after generation. Some of it came from his grandfather, maybe even his great-grandfather. The clutter could stay. Vic did not want it, did not want to sort through it; he just wanted to let it be. But the trees would remain with him and he would always mourn them. He had laboured for them all of his life. They would most likely die, although a few might remain, maybe the Black Twigs, like a tribe of vagabonds. He had seen it before; deserted properties where the house had been gone for decades, but the trees remained, obstinate apple, pear and lemon trees that would not yield. He thought of the desperado.

He went beyond the orchard to where the patches of blackberry bushes reached out for his legs. There were rabbit droppings and tunnels that led to burrows that had been here since the area was first discovered. The rabbits would outlast everyone, everything. Nothing could drive them away; there was no predator, no virus, nothing. He continued on to the rail cutting and further to where the station house had always been. Now there was just an oddly shaped mound, covered by thick grass. Vic sat down and looked up at the bland sky that promised rain.

He would never come back here. This place would fall into some corner of his mind and it would, he knew, return to him only in the uncertainty of sleep from which he would wake and stare into the night. He waited until the storm came, until he felt it soak through his clothes, until his hands were bleached. Then, he lay down on the ground and wanted to scream, but when he opened his mouth there was nothing, just as it had been when he was a child. He heard himself weeping, then crying and he hugged his knees close to his chest.

— ★ —

Jane left for Bendigo, took the girls and went while Vic waited. He cleaned the shed, sold farm machinery and counted down the days until settlement. There was more to do than he thought. He spoke to the girls on the phone, spent a weekend in Bendigo with them and they cried when he left. Word came from Violet that Edna had passed, and the funeral had already been. He stayed on the farm and left Henrithvale alone and it didn't bother him. Although, he received a letter from Brian a few days after the girls were taken out of the school and they'd left with Jane. It told Vic his membership in The Henrithvale Growers' Association had been terminated and that he had no place at the meetings, that his dishonesty and betrayal had dishonoured the legacy of his father. It said the town would prosper, would be better off, without him; he simply didn't have the courage of those that had come before. So be it. He slept on an inflated mattress in the lounge room. Sometimes at night he thought he heard ugly voices pushing up from under the floor boards. Sometimes he would call out, hoarse and desperate and then lay still with fear so strong his jaw felt as if it had locked into place. It was John's house now.

He dreamt about the Grand Final, about the final few seconds. Sometimes he caught the ball but did not know where the goals were. Other times, no matter how hard he kicked the ball it would not budge from the mud. He wanted to change the outcome, but not even his dreams would comply. His thoughts were hounded by what might have been; if only the kick had dropped short and landed in his arms, or had sat up, so he could gather and then run in and kick a goal. Maybe he should have pressed back harder, maybe he shouldn't have come so far up the ground. Maybe he should've sold the farm when John died and just been done with it then. Maybe he could've found something else. That ball. He had touched it, felt it on the tips of his fingers, could still feel it.

On the morning of settlement day, a young man in a suit knocked on the back door, and said he was to take vacant possession. Vic deflated the air mattress and packed it in the back of the ute next to a collection of tarp covered boxes. He signed the paperwork the young man had and handed him the key.

"S'pose you want me to go?" Vic said and the young man did not seem to know how to answer.

Vic sat in the ute, and the urge to run, to be somewhere spread through his veins. He took a breath, subdued the feeling and drove to where the driveway met with the road. He sat there and watched a yellow-tailed black cockatoo at rest in the updraft over the endless hills. Then suddenly it turned and disappeared towards town. Last night the old dream returned but it was only now that he recalled it. Again, he had marvelled at the vivid desert with its reddish sand, flaxen coloured grass, immense sandstone buttes and menacing blue sky. Only he was no longer standing on the veranda of the rough-hewn house watching an approaching horse and rider. Now, he was the rider. He noted a small gathering on the veranda, but his eyes were drawn to the pitch-dark that existed inside the house beyond the open door.

As he neared the house the horse stopped, and he swung out of the saddle and swaggered towards the people on the veranda. He did not recognise them but thought them familiar. One by one they turned away from him and entered the house. He came forward and stood on the veranda at the edge of the doorway, his left arm holding onto his right elbow and his shadow extending into the pitch-dark. If the people inside were looking out at him they would see none of his features, only a silhouette. He wondered if he should enter the house but then the dream ended.

Vic did not know what to make of it and turned the ute out onto the road, glancing at the rear-view mirror. His mother was on the driveway decorating the front gate with Christmas tinsel and he wasn't there to help. A long time ago she told him that sometimes you've got to live more for other people than for yourself, but that's okay because sometimes they'll do it for you too. She held up a hand as if to call him home, but smiled, gave a wave, and he drove on.

*Reading Sideways Press* is a Melbourne-based small press founded in 2018 by Nuraini Juliastuti and Andy Fuller. *Reading Sideways Press* publishes books and zines on art, sports and literature.

readingsidewayspress.com
readingsidewayspress@gmail.com